# Essentials

## *of*

# American History

*A concise survey from colonial
times to the Clinton election*

*by*
**John S. Tulp**
*(Groton School, MA)*

**WAYSIDE PUBLISHING**
www.waysidepublishing.com

ISBN 1-877653-79-9

# Table of Contents

# Preface

This book comes from the conviction that history is most exciting when its own voices reach students directly. When one has the opportunity to sift through the words of a crucial document, to read the first-hand account of an experience from the past, or to weigh the interpretation of a perceptive historian, it is hard to avoid getting caught up in the rich material that American history provides.

Many students and teachers of survey courses face the same problem: how to master the large body of factual information involved. Conventional textbooks offer thoughtful and detailed presentations of both political and social history, but these books are often enormous. Students spend so much time simply working through such texts that they don't get the opportunity to deal directly with the best primary and secondary sources. As a result, they often miss out on the excellent training in judgment and analysis that working with those sources provides.

Great American history courses are created by individual teachers and their students. The goal of this book is to enable teachers to provide the infrastructure of facts and events in American history into which may be added the primary and secondary sources that will challenge and inspire students. It is also an excellent review text for standardized tests in American history.

## To the Teacher

This book is designed to give a solid, reliable coverage of the facts of American history from the earliest settlement to the year 1992, and to do it with such brevity that the majority of your course can be devoted to interesting material from a refreshing variety of sources. With this book, you can explore topics of special interest in more depth without paying the price of gaps in the essential information of a solid survey.

When you use this text, you need to keep its goals in mind. Since this book is focused on specific facts, it gravitates toward information about political rather than social history. This does not reflect a lack of interest in history beyond the political, but the belief that those other dimensions speak best for themselves. The direct account of a settler's diary or a slave's narrative will express those experiences far more vividly than any textbook's second-hand assessment. A few pages of Emerson will make a more eloquent, thought-provoking impression than a two-sentence overview of his ideas.

This book does not present summaries of leading themes for each period that it covers. Since the information here is highly compressed and comes with a minimum of interpretive comment, a class can use discussion to formulate themes. Students could read the interpretive summary of a fine historian, or they could wrestle with the clash that comes when two able historians reach opposing conclusions from the same objective facts. Any one of these approaches is likely to be more engaging and enriching than simply taking in a textbook statement of themes as if it were fact itself.

## To the Student

Whether your history course is structured around readings from varied sources or the use of a single text, there comes a time when you must bring all the material back into focus for a comprehensive course exam, the SAT 2, or the Advanced Placement Exam. In many subjects, such tests challenge the general level of skill that you have acquired, but in history you must retain command of specific information that may not have been discussed in class for months. This can be a daunting prospect, regardless of the materials the course has been using throughout the year. Although this book was not written as a specific preparation for any national test, more than ten years of classroom use have shown that it is an extremely valuable resource to use when studying for these tests.

## Acknowledgments

Several people have given their support to producing this book. William McCook, formerly of Middlesex School, was generous with his time and insight when the material took its first form a number of years ago. John Tyler and John Lyons, both of Groton School, have given valuable assistance to its recent revision and expansion. Anne Emerson and Charlie Aldrich created the cover design. At Book Tech, Michele Barry has offered excellent advice on the final shape of the book, not to mention her astute grasp of the history itself, while Cindy Beams has been an ongoing source of encouragement and intelligent focus for the project as a whole. I have depended on their help and am very grateful to each of them.

John S. Tulp
Groton School
Groton, MA
June 2002

# Timeline of Events

**The Precolonial Period to the Revolutionary Period (1492–1763)**

| | |
|---|---|
| 1492 | Christopher Columbus lands in the Bahamas |
| 1497 | John Cabot sails to North America for England |
| 1513 | Ponce de León explores the Florida coast for Spain |
| | Vasco de Nuñez Balboa views the Pacific Ocean |
| 1518–1530 | Smallpox epidemic among Central and South American Indians |
| 1521 | Hernando Cortez conquers the Aztecs in Mexico |
| 1534 | Jacques Cartier explores the St. Lawrence River for France |
| 1535 | Francisco Pizarro conquers the Incas in Peru |
| 1585 | Sir Walter Raleigh's attempted colony at Roanoke |
| 1607 | First permanent English colony at Jamestown, Virginia |
| 1610 | Henry Hudson explores the St. Lawrence region for the Dutch |
| 1617 | First exporting of tobacco from Virginia |
| 1619 | First arrival of African laborers for sale in Virginia |
| | Establishment of the House of Burgesses |
| 1620 | Arrival of the *Mayflower* at Plymouth, Massachusetts |
| | Mayflower Compact |
| 1630 | Establishment of Massachusetts Bay Colony |
| 1632 | Founding of Maryland |
| 1635 | Roger Williams founds Rhode Island |
| 1636 | Thomas Hooker founds a settlement in Connecticut |
| 1637 | Anne Hutchinson banished from Massachusetts Bay Colony |
| | Pequot Indian War in Massachusetts |
| 1649 | Execution of Charles I in England; Stuart rule replaced by the Commonwealth |
| 1660 | Restoration of the Stuarts to the English throne |
| | First of the Navigation Acts |
| 1663 | Founding of Carolina |
| 1664 | Britain takes over New Amsterdam, establishing New York |
| 1671 | Beginning of Metacomet's War in New England |
| 1676 | Bacon's Rebellion in Virginia |
| 1679 | New Hampshire established as a royal colony |
| 1681 | Founding of Pennsylvania |
| 1686 | Formation of the Dominion of New England |

| | |
|---|---|
| 1688 | Glorious Revolution in England |
| | Leisler's Rebellion in New York |
| 1692 | Witchcraft trials in Salem, Massachusetts |
| 1730s–60s | Great Awakening |
| 1732 | Molasses Act passed by Parliament |
| 1733 | Founding of Georgia |
| 1739 | Stono slave revolt in Carolina |
| 1754 | Beginning of Seven Years' War |

**The Outbreak of the American Revolution (1763–1776)**

| | |
|---|---|
| 1763 | The Treaty of Paris |
| | The Proclamation Line of 1763 |
| 1764 | The Sugar Act |
| 1765 | The Stamp Act |
| | Organization of the Sons of Liberty |
| 1766 | The Stamp Act repealed |
| | The Declaratory Act |
| 1767 | The Townshend Acts |
| 1768 | British troops arrive in Boston |
| 1770 | The Boston Massacre |
| | Townshend Acts repealed, except for duty on tea |
| | Committees of Correspondence founded |
| 1773 | The Boston Tea Party |
| 1774 | The Coercive Acts (a.k.a. the Intolerable Acts) |
| | The Quebec Act |
| | First Continental Congress convenes in Philadelphia |
| | Declaration of Rights and Grievances passed |
| 1775 | Battles of Lexington and Concord |
| | Second Continental Congress convenes |
| | George Washington appointed commander of colonial forces |
| | The Battle of Bunker Hill (Breed's Hill) |
| | Benedict Arnold fails to seize Quebec City |
| 1776 | Thomas Paine's *Common Sense* |
| | The Declaration of Independence |

**The American Revolution (1776–1783)**

| | |
|---|---|
| 1776 | Siege of New York by British Fleet |
| | New York troops relieved by Gen. Washington in March |
| | British troops land at Staten Island in July |
| | Continental Army under Washington defeated at Brooklyn Heights (August) and White Plains (October) |
| | Continental Army defeats Hessians at Trenton (December 26) |

| 1777 | Continental Army successful at Princeton (January) |
| | Americans winter at Morristown, NJ |
| | British attempt but fail to cut off New England from remaining colonies |
| | Articles of Confederation written by Continental Congress |
| | Washington and Howe clash at Brandywine (September) and Germantown (October); British generally successful |
| | Continental forces withdraw to Valley Forge for winter |
| 1778 | Formal Treaty of alliance with France (March) |
| | British move military operations to southern colonies |
| 1779 | Spain declares war on Great Britain |
| 1780 | Continental troops defeat Tory force at King's Mountain |
| 1781 | British troops repeatedly harassed by Continental forces (Cowpens, SC—January; Guilford Court House, NC—March) |
| | Gen. Cornwallis retreats to Yorktown to await evacuation by fleet |
| | Hemmed in by combined French/American force; surrenders in October |
| 1783 | Treaty of Paris signed; hostilities officially over |

## The Era of the Articles of Confederation (1783–1789)

| 1781 | Virginia cedes its claims to western lands to federal government following similar action by other states |
| | Articles of Confederation ratified |
| 1784 | Spain closes lower Mississippi to American navigation |
| 1785 | The Land Ordinance of 1785 |
| 1786 | Shay's Rebellion in western Massachusetts |
| | Annapolis Convention held to suggest revision of Articles |
| 1787 | Northwest Ordinance of 1787 |
| | Constitutional Convention convenes in Philadelphia |
| | New Constitution written |
| | Delaware becomes first state to ratify Constitution in December |
| 1788 | Publication of the *Federalist Papers* |
| | Crucial votes for ratification in Virginia and New York |

## The Federalist Period (1789–1800)

| ♦ 1789–97 | Presidency of George Washington |
| 1789 | George Washington elected and inaugurated first president |
| | Judiciary Act of 1789 |
| | Tariff Act of 1789 |
| | French Revolution breaks out |
| 1791 | First ten amendments (the Bill of Rights) ratified |
| | Hamilton's three reports to Congress |
| | Vermont becomes the $14^{th}$ state |
| 1793 | Washington begins second term as president |
| | Citizen Genêt arrives representing new French Republic |
| | Eli Whitney invents cotton gin, also develops the concept of interchangeable parts in manufacturing |
| 1794 | Whiskey Rebellion put down |
| | British Royal Navy begins to seize American ships trading with the French West Indies |
| | Washington proclaims American neutrality in European affairs |
| 1795 | Jay's Treaty with Great Britain |
| | Pickney's Treaty with Spain |
| | Treaty of Greenville with Indians in Northwest |
| 1796 | Washington's Farewell Address |
| | John Adams elected president over Thomas Jefferson in close vote (Jefferson becomes vice president) |
| ♦ 1797–1801 | Presidency of John Adams |
| 1797 | The XYZ affair |
| 1798 | Department of Navy established |
| | Undeclared naval warfare with France |
| | Alien and Sedition Acts passed by Congress |
| | Virginia and Kentucky Resolutions |

## The Jeffersonian Era Through the War of 1812 (1800–1815)

| ♦ 1801–1809 | Presidency of Thomas Jefferson |
| 1801 | Judiciary Act of 1801—the "Midnight Appointments" |
| | John Marshall appointed Chief Justice of Supreme Court |
| 1802 | Spanish officials in New Orleans refuse to permit Americans to deposit goods there for transshipment |
| 1803 | Louisiana Territory purchased from France |
| | Supreme Court case *Marbury v. Madison* |
| | American fleet in Mediterranean reinforced |
| | Lewis and Clark expedition sets forth |

| | |
|---|---|
| 1805 | American naval forces defeat Barbary pirates |
| | Justice Chase of Supreme Court impeached but not convicted |
| | Battle of Trafalgar gains Great Britain domination of seas |
| 1806 | The Berlin Decree issued by Napoleon of France |
| 1807 | Aaron Burr tried for treason and acquitted |
| | The Milan Decree (also by France) |
| | Orders in Council by Great Britain |
| | USS *Chesapeake* boarded by English warship |
| | The Embargo Act |
| 1808 | Importation of slaves into United States prohibited |
| 1809 | Embargo Act repealed; replaced by the Nonintercourse Act |
| ◆1809–1817 | Presidency of James Madison |
| 1810 | Macon's Bill #2 |
| 1811 | "War Hawks" enter Congress |
| | Madison reinstitutes embargo against Great Britain |
| | Battle of Tippecanoe |
| 1812 | War declared against Great Britain |
| | Detroit lost to Canadian General Isaac Brock |
| 1813 | Capt. Perry victorious over British on Lake Erie |
| | British forced to abandon Detroit |
| | British tighten naval blockage of Atlantic ports |
| | Francis Cabot Lowell organizes Boston Manufacturing Company |
| 1814 | Napoleon abdicates; exiled on Elba Island |
| | British capture, burn Washington, D.C. (August) |
| | British forces marching south toward Lake Champlain turned back at Plattsburgh Bay |
| | Hartford Convention |
| | Treaty of Ghent signed ending War of 1812 |
| 1815 | Andrew Jackson successfully defends New Orleans against British |

## The "Era of Good Feelings" (1815–1824)

| | |
|---|---|
| 1815 | Madison's Annual Message to Congress proposes the "American System" |
| 1816 | The Tariff of 1816 |
| | The Second National Bank of the United States |
| ◆1817–1825 | Presidency of James Monroe |
| 1817 | The Bonus Bill of John Calhoun vetoed by Madison |
| | Rush-Bagot Agreement between U.S. and Great Britain |

| | |
|---|---|
| 1819 | Adams-Otis Treaty results in purchase of Florida from Spain |
| | Supreme Court cases: |
| | *Dartmouth College v. Woodward* |
| | *McCulloch v. Maryland* |
| 1820 | The Missouri Compromise |
| 1823 | The Monroe Doctrine proclaimed |

## John Quincy Adams and the Jacksonian Era (1824–1840)

| | |
|---|---|
| 1824 | Supreme Court case *Gibbons v. Ogden* |
| ◆1825–1829 | Presidency of John Quincy Adams |
| 1825 | Erie Canal completed |
| 1828 | Tariff of 1828 (a.k.a. the Tariff of Abominations) |
| | Election of 1828 (Jackson elected) |
| | John Calhoun introduces the theory of "nullification" in the South Carolina Exposition and Protest |
| ◆1829–1837 | Presidency of Andrew Jackson |
| 1829 | Jackson institutes the Spoils System of office rotation |
| 1830 | The Webster-Haynes Debate |
| | The Indian Land Removal Act |
| 1831 | William Lloyd Garrison first publishes "The Liberator" |
| | Nat Turner's Revolt in Virginia |
| | Supreme Court case *Worcester v. George* |
| 1832 | Tariff of 1832; South Carolina nullifies tariff |
| | Jackson overwhelmingly reelected; removes federal funds from National Bank |
| 1833 | Compromise tariff measure devised by Henry Clay |
| | The Force Bill |
| 1836 | Specie Circular |
| | Texas declares independence from Mexico; applies for annexation to U.S.; application denied |
| | Gag Laws instituted in Congress |
| ◆1837–1841 | Presidency of Martin Van Buren |
| 1837 | Recession of 1837; lasts for several years |
| 1839 | The Aroostook War |
| 1840 | Election of 1840 ("Tippecanoe and Tyler Too") |

## Expansion and Social Reform (1840–1850)

| | |
|---|---|
| ◆1841 | Presidency of William Henry Harrison |
| | Harrison dies suddenly; replaced by John Tyler |
| | Tyler vetoes bills establishing national bank, internal improvements |
| ◆1841–1845 | Presidency of John Tyler |

| | |
|---|---|
| 1842 | The Webster-Ashburton Treaty |
| 1844 | Treaty to admit Texas to Union defeated in Senate |
| ♦1845–1849 | Presidency of James Polk |
| 1845 | Texas admitted to statehood within Union |
| | Widespread support for America's Manifest Destiny |
| 1846 | Treaty with Great Britain settles northern border of Oregon Territory |
| | Mexican-American War begins |
| | Wilmot Proviso proposed in Congress |
| 1847 | Mormons under Brigham Young settle in Utah Territory |
| | Santa Fe and California occupied by Union troops |
| 1848 | Treaty of Guadalupe Hidalgo ends Mexican-American War |
| | Free-Soil Party formed |
| | Seneca Falls Convention |
| | Gold discovered at Sutter's Mill in California; the gold rush begins |
| ♦1849–1850 | Presidency of Zachary Taylor |

## Prelude to Civil War (1850–1861)

| | |
|---|---|
| 1850 | Taylor dies; replaced by Millard Fillmore |
| | Compromise of 1850 agreed upon |
| ♦1850–1853 | Presidency of Millard Fillmore |
| 1852 | Publication of *Uncle Tom's Cabin* |
| | The American Party (a.k.a. the Know-Nothings) appears |
| ♦1853–1857 | Presidency of Franklin Pierce |
| 1853 | The Gadsden Purchase |
| 1854 | The Kansas-Nebraska Act ("Popular Sovereignty") |
| | The Ostend Manifesto |
| | Formation of the Republican Party |
| 1856 | The Sack of Lawrence leads to "Bleeding Kansas" |
| | Charles Sumner attacked on floor of Senate |
| ♦1857–1861 | Presidency of James Buchanan |
| 1857 | Supreme Court case *Dred Scott v. Sanford* |
| | Congress rejects the Lecompton Constitution for Kansas |
| 1858 | The Lincoln-Douglas debates produce the Freeport Doctrine |
| 1859 | John Brown's raid on federal arsenal at Harper's Ferry, Virginia |
| 1860 | Election of 1860 (Lincoln elected) |
| | South Carolina votes to secede; Deep South follows |
| ♦1861–1865 | Presidency of Abraham Lincoln |
| 1861 | The Crittenden Amendments unsuccessful |

## The Civil War (1861–1865)

| | |
|---|---|
| 1861 | Fort Sumter fired upon |
| | Lincoln calls out state militias, expands fleet, suspends *habeas corpus* in border states |
| | First Battle at Manassas (Bull Run) |
| | The Trent Affair |
| 1862 | Homestead Act |
| | Battle of Shiloh (Capt. Farragut seizes New Orleans) |
| | The Peninsular Campaign in Virginia |
| | Slavery abolished in District of Columbia |
| | Second Battle at Manassas (Bull Run) |
| | Battle of Antietam |
| 1863 | The Emancipation Proclamation |
| | Battle of Chancellorsville |
| | Battle of Gettysburg |
| | Battle of Vicksburg |
| | Battle of Chattanooga |
| | Lincoln announces his Proclamation of Amnesty and Reconstruction (the "Ten Percent Plan") |
| 1864 | Wade-Davis Bill for Reconstruction passed by Congress |
| | Sherman's March to the Sea |
| | Lincoln wins reelection with 55 percent majority |
| 1865 | Lee surrenders to Grant at Appomattox Court House |
| | Lincoln assassinated (April 14); Andrew Johnson becomes president |

## The Period of Reconstruction (1865–1877)

| | |
|---|---|
| ♦1865–1869 | Presidency of Andrew Johnson |
| 1865 | The Freedmen's Bureau created by Congress |
| | Southern States enact Black Codes |
| | Congress refuses to accept Louisiana back into Union under Ten Percent Plan |
| | President Johnson accepts principle of Ten Percent Plan; southern states reorganize under plan |
| | Thirteenth Amendment proposed and ratified |
| 1866 | Fourteenth Amendment proposed (ratified in 1868) |
| | Ku Klux Klan founded |
| 1867 | First Reconstruction Act passed over Johnson's veto |
| | Tenure of Office Act passed |
| | Beginning of the reservation system for American Indians |
| | Patrons of Husbandry (Grange) founded |

| | |
|---|---|
| 1868 | President Johnson impeached but not convicted |
| | Ulysses S. Grant elected president |
| | Purchase of Alaska from Russia ("Seward's Folly") |
| 1869 | Fifteenth Amendment proposed (ratified in 1870) |
| | Completion of first transcontinental railroad |
| | Knights of Labor founded |
| ♦ 1869–1877 | Presidency of Ulysses S. Grant |
| 1872 | Amnesty Act |
| 1873 | Recession hits country |
| | All currency ordered backed by gold |
| 1874 | Discovery of gold in Black Hills (South Dakota) |
| 1875 | Civil Rights Act of 1875 |
| | Trial of Molly McGuires |
| 1876 | Disputed election of 1876 (Hayes v. Tilden) |
| | Battle of Little Bighorn; defeat of Seventh Cavalry |
| | Supreme Court case *Munn v. Illinois* |
| ♦ 1877–1881 | Presidency of Rutherford B. Hayes |
| 1877 | Hayes removes remaining Union troops from South, ending Reconstruction |

## The Gilded Age and U.S. Imperialism (1878–1900)

| | |
|---|---|
| 1878 | Bland-Allison Act |
| | U.S. receives a naval base in Pago Pago (Samoa) |
| ♦ 1881 | Presidency of James Garfield |
| | American Federation of Labor founded |
| | James Garfield assassinated |
| ♦ 1881–1885 | Presidency of Chester A. Arthur |
| 1882 | Standard Oil Company trust formed by John D. Rockefeller |
| 1883 | Pendleton Act (Civil Service) |
| ♦ 1885–1889 | Presidency of Grover Cleveland (first administration) |
| 1886 | Haymarket Massacre |
| 1887 | Dawes Act |
| | Interstate Commerce Act |
| ♦ 1889–1893 | Presidency of Benjamin Harrison |
| 1890 | Frederick Jackson Turner publishes "Frontier Theory" |
| | Battle of Wounded Knee |
| | McKinley Tariff |
| | Sherman Silver Purchase Act |
| | Sherman Anti-Trust Act |
| 1892 | Homestead Strike |
| | Populist Party founded in Omaha |
| ♦ 1893–1897 | Presidency of Grover Cleveland (second administration) |
| 1893 | Recession hits country |
| | Sherman Silver Purchase Act repealed |

| | |
|---|---|
| | Queen Liliuokalani of Hawaii overthrown |
| 1894 | Pullman Strike |
| 1895 | Outbreak of Cuban revolt against Spanish rule |
| 1896 | Supreme Court case *Plessy v. Ferguson* |
| | National Association of Colored Women founded |
| | Election of 1896 (McKinley v. Bryan) |
| ♦ 1897–1901 | Presidency of William McKinley |
| 1897 | Spanish agree to limited self-rule in Cuba |
| 1898 | Hawaii annexed to the United States |
| | U.S. battleship *Maine* sunk in Havana Harbor |
| | Beginning of Spanish-American War |
| | Formation of the Anti-Imperialist League |
| 1899 | Reform mayors elected in Toledo, Detroit, and Galveston |
| 1900 | Open Door policy in China announced by Secretary of State John Hays |

## Progressivism and World War I (1901–1920)

| | |
|---|---|
| ♦ 1901–1909 | Presidency of Theodore Roosevelt |
| 1901 | U.S. Steel Company formed; first billion-dollar corporation |
| | Hay-Pauncefote Treaty gives United States right to build canal |
| 1902 | Filipino rebels in Philippines give in to American rule |
| 1903 | Successful revolt of Panama against Columbia |
| 1904 | Great Northern Securities Corporation dissolved under Anti-Trust Law |
| | Roosevelt Corollary to the Monroe Doctrine announced |
| 1905 | Portsmouth Peace Conference between Russia and Japan |
| 1906 | Hepburn Act |
| 1907 | Gentlemen's Agreement between United States and Japan |
| | Recession hits country (Panic of 1907) |
| 1908 | Root-Takahira Agreement |
| ♦ 1909–1913 | Presidency of William Howard Taft |
| 1909 | Payne-Aldrich Tariff |
| 1910 | Democrats gain control of House of Representatives |
| 1912 | U.S. Marines intervene in Nicaragua |
| ♦ 1913–1921 | Presidency of Woodrow Wilson |
| 1913 | Sixteenth Amendment permits graduated income tax |
| | Seventeenth Amendment provides for popular election of Senators |
| | Federal Reserve Act |
| | Underwood-Simmons Tariff |
| | Report of the Pujo Committee |

| | |
|---|---|
| 1914 | Clayton Anti-Trust Act |
| | World War I breaks out in Europe |
| | U.S. forces seize port of Vera Cruz in Mexico |
| 1915 | *Lusitania* sinks with substantial loss of civilian life |
| 1916 | Keating-Owen Act |
| | American troops chase Pancho Villa into Mexico |
| | Sussex Pledge by Germany promises end to unrestricted submarine attacks |
| 1917 | Russian Revolution |
| | Germany reinstitutes unrestricted submarine warfare |
| | Publication of the Zimmermann Telegram |
| | United States enters World War I on side of the allies |
| | Fourteen Points issued by Wilson |
| | Selective Service Act |
| | Espionage Act |
| | Trading with the Enemy Act |
| 1918 | Sedition Act |
| | Armistice agreed to by Germans |
| 1919 | Versailles Treaty revealed |
| | Boston police strike put down by Gov. Calvin Coolidge |
| | Race riots in various U.S. cities |

## The Twenties (1920–1929)

| | |
|---|---|
| 1920 | United States Senate refuses to ratify Versailles Treaty |
| | Sacco and Vanzetti arrested for armed robbery and murder |
| | Eighteenth Amendment establishes Prohibition |
| | Nineteenth Amendment guarantees Women's Suffrage |
| ♦1921–1923 | Presidency of Warren G. Harding |
| 1921–1922 | Washington Arms Conference |
| 1921 | Separate Peace Treaty signed between United States and Germany |
| 1922 | Fordney-McCumber Tariff |
| 1923 | Teapot Dome and other scandals revealed |
| ♦1923–1929 | Presidency of Calvin Coolidge |
| 1924 | Adjusted Compensation Act (the "Bonus Bill") |
| 1927 | Introduction of sound motion pictures |
| 1928 | Briand-Kellogg Pact |

## Depression and the New Deal (1929–1939)

| | |
|---|---|
| ♦1929–1933 | Presidency of Herbert Hoover |
| 1929 | Stock market crash |
| 1930 | Hawley-Smoot Tariff |
| | London Arms Conference |
| 1931 | Japan invades Manchuria |
| 1932 | Reconstruction Finance Corporation |
| | Federal Home Loan Bank Act |
| ♦1933–1945 | Presidency of Franklin D. Roosevelt |
| 1933 | The "First Hundred Days" |
| | Twenty-First Amendment repeals Prohibition |
| | Emergency Banking Act |
| | Glass-Steagall Act |
| | Gold Reserve Act |
| | Federal Emergency Relief Administration |
| | Agricultural Adjustment Act |
| | Indian Reorganization Act |
| | Home Owners Loan Corporation |
| | National Industrial Recovery Act |
| | Tennessee Valley Authority |
| | Adolf Hitler gains control of German government |
| | U.S. troops removed from Haiti |
| 1934 | Timetable for Philippine independence agreed to |
| 1935 | National Industrial Recovery Act declared unconstitutional |
| | The "Second Hundred Days" |
| | Works Projects Administration |
| | Huey Long of Louisiana assassinated |
| | Social Security Act |
| | National Industrial Recovery Administration declared unconstitutional |
| | Committee for Industrial Organization (CIO) formed |
| | Public Works Administration |
| | Italy invades Ethiopia |
| | Report of the Nye Committee |
| | First Neutrality Act |
| 1936 | Civil War breaks out in Spain |
| | Hitler takes over the Rhineland |
| | Agricultural Adjustment Act declared unconstitutional |
| | Second Neutrality Act |
| 1937 | Roosevelt suggests adding up to six additional justices to Supreme Court |
| | Recession hits country |
| | Japan invades China |
| | Third Neutrality Act |
| 1938 | Second Agricultural Adjustment Act |
| | Fair Labor Standards Act |
| | Republicans, southern Democrats make gains in Congressional elections |
| | Hitler creates union with Austria |
| | Munich Agreement concedes Sudetenland to Germany |

## World War II (1939–1945)

| | |
|---|---|
| 1939 | Germany signs nonaggression pact with Soviet Union |
| | Germany invades Poland; World War II begins |
| 1940 | Roosevelt exchanges destroyers for British naval bases |
| | France falls to Germany |
| | Italy, under Mussolini, joins Germany in war |
| | U.S. embargoes war materials going to Japan |
| 1941 | Lend-Lease Act |
| | Roosevelt announces the Atlantic Charter |
| | Germany invades Soviet Union |
| | Japanese raid on Pearl Harbor; U.S. enters the war on side of Allies |
| 1942 | North African campaign |
| | Battles of Coral Sea and Midway |
| 1943 | German North African army surrenders |
| | Allied invasion of Italy |
| | Casablanca Conference |
| 1944 | Normandy invasion |
| | Battle of the Bulge |
| | Supreme Court refuses to block relocation of Japanese Americans |
| | G. I. Bill |
| ♦1945–1953 | Presidency of Harry S Truman |
| 1945 | Yalta Conference |
| | Germany accepts unconditional surrender |
| | Iwo Jima, Okinawa taken in fierce fighting |
| | Potsdam Conference |
| | Atomic bombs dropped on Hiroshima and Nagasaki |
| | Japan accepts unconditional surrender |
| | United Nations formed |

## Truman and the Beginning of the Cold War (1945–1960)

| | |
|---|---|
| 1946 | Baruch Plan proposed |
| | Employment Act |
| | Taft-Hartley Act |
| | Security checks of government employees begun |
| 1947 | George Kennan publicizes "Containment Theory" |
| | Truman Doctrine announced |
| | Marshall Plan announced |
| | National Security Act |
| 1948 | Berlin Blockade by Soviet Union |
| | Alger Hiss treason trial |
| | Israel founded in Palestinian territory |
| | Truman's surprise victory over Thomas Dewey |
| 1949 | Soviet Union explodes first atomic bomb |

| | |
|---|---|
| | Klaus Fuchs revealed to have given Soviet Union secret nuclear information |
| | North Atlantic Treaty Organization (NATO) formed |
| | Nationalist Chinese defeated by Communists under Mao Zedong |
| 1950 | Alger Hiss convicted of perjury |
| | Joseph McCarthy alleges Communists in State Department |
| | McCarran Internal Security Act |
| | Document NSC-68 |
| | North Korean invasion of South Korea |
| | Chinese join fighting when U.S. troops move into North Korea |
| 1951 | Gen. Douglas MacArthur relieved of command by President Truman |
| | Twenty-Second Amendment prohibits more than two terms as president |
| ♦1953–1961 | Presidency of Dwight D. Eisenhower |
| 1953 | Discovery of genetic transmission by DNA |
| | Joseph Stalin dies; replaced by Georgi Malenkof |
| | Execution of Julius and Ethyl Rosenberg |
| | Truce signed in Korea at Punmunjom |
| 1954 | Supreme Court case *Brown v. Board of Education of Topeka* |
| | Restoration of West German sovereignty |
| | Fall of Dien Bien Phu to Viet Minh under Ho Chi Minh |
| | Geneva Conference agrees to temporary division of Vietnam |
| | Army/McCarthy hearings televised |
| | Senator Joseph McCarthy censured by Senate |
| | Southeast Asia Treaty Organization (SEATO) founded |
| 1955 | Geneva Convention |
| | AF of L and CIO merge |
| | Baghdad Pact signed |
| | Neo Dinh Diem wins presidential election in South Vietnam |
| | Egypt and Soviet Union sign arms deal |
| | Bus boycott in Montgomery, Alabama |
| | Polio vaccine put into use |
| 1956 | Interstate Highway Act |
| | Hungarian Revolution put down by Soviet Union |
| | Egypt nationalizes Suez Canal |
| | Israel, France, Great Britain invade Egypt over canal |
| | Chinese shelling of Quemoy, Matse |
| 1957 | President Eisenhower uses federal troops to enforce desegregation |
| | Eisenhower Doctrine announced for Middle East |
| | Recession hits country |
| | *Sputnik* launched by Soviet Union |

| | |
|---|---|
| 1958 | Natl. Aeronautics and Space Agency (NASA) founded |
| | V. P. Nixon mobbed in South America |
| 1959 | Nikita Khruschev visits the U.S. |
| | Fidel Castro seizes control of Cuba |
| 1960 | U-2 spy plane shot down while over USSR |
| | Paris Summit Conference breaks down |

## "New Frontier," "Great Society," and Vietnam (1960-1968)

| | |
|---|---|
| ◆1961-1963 | Presidency of John F. Kennedy |
| 1961 | U.S. severs relations with Cuba |
| | Bay of Pigs invasion |
| | Alliance for Progress |
| | Peace Corps |
| | Housing Act of 1961 |
| | Summit meeting in Vienna between Kennedy and Khruschev |
| | Soviet cosmonaut placed into orbit |
| | Berlin Wall constructed |
| | U.S. resumes underground testing of nuclear weapons |
| | 23rd Amendment grants "home-rule" to Washington, DC |
| 1962 | Steel industry repeals price increases |
| | Cuban Missile Crisis |
| | Port Huron Statement founding SDJ |
| 1963 | Washington rally for civil rights addressed by Dr. Martin Luther King |
| | U.S./USSR agreed to prohibit atmospheric testing of nuclear weapons |
| | First Clean Air Act |
| | Kennedy assassinated in Dallas |
| 1963-1969 | Presidency of Lyndon B. Johnson |
| 1964 | Medicare/Social Security Bill |
| | Elementary & Secondary Education Act |
| | 24th Amendment prohibits poll tax |
| | Civil Rights Act of 1964 prohibits discrimination in public accommodations and private employment |
| | Free speech movement at Berkeley |
| | Gulf of Tonkin Resolution passed |
| 1965 | Immigration Act ends quota system |
| | Cesar Chavez begins organization of migrant farm labor |
| | Civil Rights Act provides for federal inspection of voting registration |
| | Racial unrest in Watts and Selma, AL |
| | President Diem of South Vietnam overthrown by Thieu |
| | Massive increase in U.S. troops for Vietnam |
| 1966 | Department of Transportation created |
| | Natl. Organization of Women organized |

| | |
|---|---|
| | Race riots in Chicago and Cleveland |
| 1967 | U.S. population passes 200 million mark |
| | Race riot in Detroit |
| 1968 | Commission on Civil Disorders reports |
| | Dr. Martin Luther King assassinated |
| | Civil Rights Act prohibits discrimination in housing |
| | Tet Offensive in South Vietnam |
| | President Johnson ends bombings, calls for negotiations, announces will not run for reelection |
| | Robert Kennedy assassinated in Calif. |
| | Democratic Natl. Convention in Chicago |

## The Nixon Presidency and its Aftermath (1968-76)

| | |
|---|---|
| ◆1969-1974 | Presidency of Richard M. Nixon |
| 1969 | American Indians seize Alcatraz Prison |
| 1969-1972 | Policy of "Vietnamization" |
| 1969 | War Moratorium march in Washington |
| 1970 | National Guard fires on war protesters at Kent State University |
| 1972 | Break-in at the Watergate Hotel |
| 1973 | Supreme Court case *Roe vs. Wade* |
| 1974 | Resignation of President Nixon |
| ◆1974 1976 | Presidency of Gerald Ford |

## From Carter to Reagan ( 1976-1980)

| | |
|---|---|
| ◆1976-1980 | Presidency of Jimmy Carter |
| 1977 | OPEC oil price hikes |
| 1978 | Supreme Court case *Bakke v. Regents of the University of California* |
| 1979 | Camp David agreement |
| | Failure of Salt II treaty |
| | Hostages taken at U.S. Embassy in Teheran, Iran |
| 1980 | Election of Ronald Reagan |

## Reagan and Bush (1980-1992)

| | |
|---|---|
| ◆1980-1988 | Presidency of Ronald Reagan |
| 1981ff | Policy of "supply-side economics" |
| | Air Traffic Controllers Union strike |
| | Attack on marines in Lebanon |
| | Support for Contras in Nicaragua |
| | Strategic Defense Initiative (SDI) proposed |
| 1986 | Iran-Contra Scandal |
| 1987 | Supreme Court confirmation hearings for Robert J. Bork |
| ◆1988-1992 | Presidency of George Bush |
| | Fall of Soviet Union |
| | Deposing of Gen. Noriega in Panama |
| 1990-1991 | Gulf War |
| 1992 | Rodney King verdict |
| | Presidential election of Bill Clinton |

# The Precolonial Period to the Revolutionary Period (1492–1763)

## Early Exploration and Conquest

The first inhabitants of North America crossed from Asia over 30,000 years ago, along a land bridge now submerged by the Bering Sea. They populated the continent with hundreds of tribes, living with distinct cultures based on differences in local geography, climate, and evolved traditions. America may have been reached by ship before **Christopher Columbus's** landing in the Bahamas in 1492. There is particularly strong evidence that Vikings under **Leif Erikson** reached the northern tip of Newfoundland before that time. However, Columbus's voyage proved decisive in opening up contact between American and European cultures.

Columbus's voyages inaugurated the Spanish conquest of a vast area from the southern part of North America, through Central America, and well into South America. By 1513, **Ponce de León** was exploring the Florida coast, and in that same year, **Vasco Nuñez de Balboa** crossed the Isthmus of Panama to view the Pacific Ocean. The primary goal of the conquest was the pursuit of gold and silver, which the Spaniards found in abundance in Mexico and South America. It was sent back in annual shipments to Spain throughout the sixteenth century, making Spain by far the wealthiest nation in Europe at that time.

In 1521, **Hernando Cortez** subdued the Aztecs in Mexico, and **Francisco Pizarro** did the same to the Incas in Peru in 1535. Though both were greatly outnumbered by the Indians they confronted, several factors made it possible for these conquistadors with their small forces to conquer such powerful Indian nations. They had certain advantages of weaponry and military organization, but they also had a psychological advantage over the Indians, who considered their arrival by sea miraculous and were particularly intimidated by the strange horses they rode. The Spanish also received crucial aid from smaller local tribes happy to help topple their powerful neighbors.

By far the most powerful ally of the conquistadors, however, was disease. Smallpox, measles, and other European diseases attacked Indians, who had no immunity to such germs. Between 1518 and 1530, a smallpox epidemic decimated Indian populations in Central and South America, and it was these weakened tribes that confronted Cortez and Pizarro. As an index of the horrible impact of European diseases, when Columbus reached the island of Hispaniola, it had a population of approximately one million Indians. Within 50 years, that number had shrunk to a few thousand.

The mentality of the Europeans was such that they could not appreciate the Indian cultures they encountered, even though the Indian cultures were often highly sophisticated. The Mayans living around Mexico's Yucatan Peninsula had developed the mathematics to produce a calendar more accurate than any used in Europe at that time. The Aztec nation had a population far in excess of the entire Indian population of North America above the Rio Grande, and its capital, Tenochtitlan, was then one of the largest, most magnificently laid out cities in the world.

Other nations soon followed Spain's lead. **Jacques Cartier** explored the St. Lawrence River for France in 1534, followed a hundred years later by **Samuel de Champlain**. **Henry Hudson** sailed the same waters for the Dutch in 1610. These men were looking for the elusive **Northwest Passage**, which, if it had existed, would have offered direct sea trade between Europe and China. In 1497, **John Cabot** made a voyage to North America for England, but England pulled out of such projects until late in the following century because the nation's economy was not strong enough to support such exploration.

The European nations made different uses of the New World. The Spanish built up a sparsely populated but tightly organized empire centered around the use of forced Indian labor to extract gold and silver. Jesuit missionaries were busily engaged there in the effort to convert the Indians to Christianity and had a more sympathetic understanding of their culture than the secular leaders. Jesuits were also active in New France, while the government's primary concern was to develop the north woods fur trade. The Dutch were interested in establishing stations for their network of global trade. Though late to enter the North American theater, England always emphasized solid residential settlements. Over time, this approach gave England a stronger hold in North America than any of its rival nations.

## Settlement of Virginia and Maryland

The first English settlement in North America was a colony on **Roanoke Island** off the coast of Virginia, organized by **Sir Walter Raleigh** and established in 1585. Lack of adequate resources and troubled relations with the Indians of the area doomed the project. When a relief expedition landed at Roanoke in 1591, there was no trace of any of the settlers.

In 1607, the Virginia Company established a colony at **Jamestown**. Though it was to become England's first permanent settlement in the New World, its early years were precarious. Of 144 men and boys who sailed from England, only 104 arrived alive at Virginia, and of these only 38 were still alive 9 months later. The members of this expedition were ill-prepared to fend for themselves. Many were disinclined to do the physical work involved, and all were vulnerable to malaria and other diseases. Plus, an overwhelming majority of men in the population made the colony inherently unstable as a community. A military type of discipline imposed by **Captain John Smith** barely saved the colony in 1608. During the "starving times" of 1609–1610, disease and malnutrition continued to take a frightful toll, despite the arrival of over 900 new settlers. Fewer than one person in ten survived.

In 1617, the Virginia Company, in its efforts to stabilize a population and assure a reliable labor force, instituted the **headright system**. New settlers who could pay their own passage were promised 50 acres of land. Those who financed the passage of poorer laborers received a headright grant for each of them, to be awarded when their terms as **indentured servants** were completed. This proved a powerful incentive for migration from England to Virginia. As a further inducement for settlement, the Company in 1619 allowed Virginians to elect delegates to the **House of Burgesses**, which became the first representative assembly in North America.

Two factors saved the endangered Virginia colony: tobacco and the aid of the Algonkian chief, **Powhattan**. The head of a confederacy of tribes and intent on subduing others, Powhattan saw the European immigrants as potential allies in his struggles against other Indian groups rather than as a force fundamentally opposed to Indian culture in general. After Powhattan's death, his brother **Opechancanough** sensed the error of this view and led an attack on the Virginia settlements in 1622. His initial massacre of colonists was devastating, though eventually he and his people succumbed to a series of military expeditions by the Englishmen. The shock of this conflict had direct effects in London. The Virginia Company, which had never realized any profit from the colony from the start, went bankrupt. King James I revoked its charter, and Virginia became a **royal colony**, under direct governance of the Crown.

Tobacco proved to be the economic salvation of the Virginia colony. First planted there by **John Rolfe** in 1611, it was exported to England six years later. By the 1620s, European smokers had created a steady demand for tobacco. As the tobacco industry grew, the colony adopted different systems to solve the problem of needed labor. One of these, the system of indenture mentioned earlier, was effective to a limited degree; however, the grueling conditions of work for an indentured servant, usually a male between the ages of 15 and 25, made it an ongoing source of social tension. The other system, far more enduring in its legacy, was slavery. In 1619, a Dutch ship sailed up Chesapeake Bay, offering African laborers for sale. The slave trade from western Africa to the West Indies grew steadily from that point, with Africans suffering horrible conditions on the **Middle Passage**, as that voyage was called. The actual status of the purchased Africans remained ambiguous through much of the seventeenth century. Some evidence shows them treated purely as slaves, while at other times they appear to have had the status of laborers with certain civil rights. By the 1680s, however, the mold had hardened, and slavery was a clearly established institution in Virginia.

The success of tobacco in Virginia inspired further colonization in the Chesapeake area. In 1632, Maryland was founded by **Cecilius Calvert**, **Lord Baltimore**. It was a **proprietary colony**, which meant that it had been given to Calvert as his own possession, to manage as he saw fit. His original intent was to govern autocratically, but pressures from the policies evolving nearby in Virginia forced him to modify that position, particularly in granting a legislative assembly similar to the House of Burgesses.

Social and political conditions in Virginia remained unsettled through the seventeenth century, as evidenced by **Bacon's Rebellion** in 1676. This sordid episode began as an avoidable conflict with the Susquehannock Indian tribe but expanded into the indiscriminate killing of Indians from all of the region's tribes, as racial hatred mingled with the desire for land. On another level, it became a power struggle between Governor George Berkeley and newcomers led by Nathaniel Bacon, who was able to inflame the anger of western settlers against Berkeley's established tidewater society.

The eighteenth century presented quite a different picture. Alarmed by the spectre of lower-class white rebellion such as they had seen in Bacon's Rebellion, well-to-do whites sought to unify their own race, placing a greater distance between themselves and black slave labor. Within their own group, poor whites deferred to the decisions and guidance offered by the wealthier families, the gentry. In return, they received certain political rights as well as practical assistance in such areas as business affairs or legal matters. Thus slavery became embedded in Virginia as the foundation not only of its agricultural economy but its social harmony as well.

## Colonial New England

The New England coast was known to fishermen during the late sixteenth century, but the first English settlement there began when the *Mayflower* landed at Plymouth in 1620. The organizers of this group were the Pilgrims or, as they called themselves, **Separatists**. They were Protestants seeking a safe haven for their religious beliefs by detaching themselves from the Church of England, away from the harassment of King James I. The Separatists, under the leadership of **William Bradford**, comprised only a third of the *Mayflower's* passengers. While still aboard ship, anticipating some social tension in the settlement they were about to found, the passengers drew up and signed the **Mayflower Compact**, an early instance of self-government in North America that also set a tone for social order in New England quite different from the conditions then prevailing in Virginia.

In 1630, the Puritans, another group of Protestant settlers, reached Massachusetts under the leadership of **John Winthrop** and the auspices of the Massachusetts Bay Company. King James I had been openly hostile to Puritanism, and his son Charles I was even more so. The Puritans objected bitterly to the policies of Charles's Archbishop, William Laud. Whereas the Separatists sought only a safe place to practice their religion, the Puritans intended to distance themselves from religious corruption in England in order to purify church practices and then bring these reforms back to the church at home. As years passed, the mission of a return to England faded, but the intensity of their own religious mission in America remained. As John Winthrop had said in a sermon aboard ship before reaching Boston, "We shall be as a city upon a hill; the eyes of all people are upon us." From the start, the Massachusetts Bay Colony had greater resources and grew more dynamically than the settlement at Plymouth, which was absorbed into the larger Massachusetts colony in 1691.

Issues of religious vision among the Massachusetts Puritans quickly became intertwined with issues of social control. The intentions of the colony's leaders were sometimes at odds with the sense of openness, both physical and psychological, inspired by their new North American setting. The leaders' desire to control village life, for example, came into frequent conflict with the settlers' desire to move out into what they perceived as freely available land. There were theological challenges, too. A young preacher named **Roger Williams** emerged as a dissident voice that would not be stilled by threat or persuasion. When he learned in 1635 that he was about to be deported back to England, he fled to the south and founded the colony of Rhode Island. In 1636, discontented with certain religious practices in Massachusetts and attracted by land itself, **Thomas Hooker** led a group of followers away and founded a colony in Connecticut.

More disturbing than either of these, however, was **Anne Hutchinson**. In 1634, she began to object to the sermons of the religious leaders of the community, insisting that God's gifts were instilled mystically into each individual, a doctrine known as **Antinomianism**. Though lacking any formal theological training, she began conducting religious gatherings in her home, attracting a strong following of many women, but also men disaffected with the colony's leadership. In 1637, Hutchinson faced trial and, in the last month of a pregnancy, was banished to Rhode Island. Her clash with the authorities gives an example of the way issues of religion, government, and gender became interwoven in Massachusetts Bay. As one of the judges said to her, "You have bine [*sic*] a Husband rather than a Wife, and a preacher rather than a Hearer, and a Magistrate rather than a subject." Another woman, **Mary Dyer**, was also condemned in Massachusetts. After following Hutchinson to Rhode Island, she subsequently became a convert to Quakerism. When she returned to Boston in 1659 to preach this faith, she was publicly hanged.

One consistent pattern between early Virginia and early Massachusetts was friction with the Indians of the region, even though in each case the English were initially dependent on Indian help for survival. In 1616, European fishermen introduced smallpox into the New England coastal tribes, which had no immunity to the germ. The disease swept through the Indian population, and English settlers arrived to find a largely depopulated coastline. Initially this enabled them to expand their landholding with little friction, but that ceased when they encountered the powerful **Pequot** tribe, which had not been touched by the epidemic. In 1637, the Massachusetts Bay Colony undertook a war against the Pequots and, with the help of the Narragansetts to the south, effectively exterminated the tribe. The Indians of coastal New England made the same error that Powhattan had made earlier in Virginia, viewing Englishmen as potential allies in conflicts among themselves rather than as a threat to all of them collectively. In 1671, a Wampanoag chief named **Metacomet** (called King Phillip by the English) tried to reverse this trend and unite all the regional tribes in a war against the Whites. The tide of events moved with him until 1675, as his forces spread through Massachusetts and Rhode Island. Within the next year, though, the movement unraveled as a result of disease, lack of food, and tribal dissent. Metacomet's War ended with his death in battle in 1676, and Indian influence in the area faded.

As in Virginia, the New England settlers initially encountered difficult conditions, and the mortality rate in their first years was high. However, they recovered quickly. The climate, though harsh, also proved healthful; and while their economy lacked a spectacular export crop like tobacco, its balance among agriculture, fishing, and lumbering gave them a solid base on which to build community life. Unlike the nearly all-male population of early Virginia, New Englanders from the start immigrated as families, a fact that had enormous influence on the patterns of settlement that evolved. Whereas the broad tidewater plain of the Chesapeake region favored individual, widely scattered farms, New England's geography combined with the mentality of its settlers to emphasize life in small, tightly integrated towns.

New England villages centered around a meetinghouse, which served both religious and civic functions. Villagers typically housed themselves in a compact area, going out each day to work in outlying fields and grazing livestock on a common pasture. These villages present a blend of authoritarianism and incipient democracy. A village could not be started without an official grant from the General Court in Boston, but once founded it could operate with considerable autonomy. Village leaders often sought to exert firm control, yet the right to vote was extended to all property-owning adult male church members. When land was parceled out at the founding of a town, it was given in proportion to each person's wealth, thus continuing the existing social hierarchy. However, this was tempered by a pervasive ethic of community contribution. As one town covenant put it, "From each according to his ability; to each as need shall require."

## The Carolinas and Georgia

In 1663, Charles II gave a large tract of land south of Virginia to a group of his supporters as a proprietary colony, which they named Carolina in his honor. Seeking to move away from England's recent social and political upheavals, they tried to establish in their colony a return to the principles of feudalism. With the help of the young philosopher **John Locke**, they drew up the **Fundamental Constitutions of Carolina** in 1669, outlining a complex government that limited political rights and patterns of land use, while guaranteeing that 40 percent of the land would always remain in the hands of a hereditary aristocracy. A system that seemed so attractive to a group of London planners never became a reality in America. Settlers simply disregarded the restrictions intended for their land use and refused to accept the Fundamental Constitutions as their form of government. Faced with such opposition, the proprietors withdrew their attempt to channel the colony's development.

The differing geography of the northern and southern regions of Carolina influenced their settlement. In the lowlands of the south, the number of slaves quickly grew to become a majority of the colony's population. (The tensions of South Carolina's slave-based society would erupt in the **Stono Rebellion** of 1739, the largest slave revolt of the colonial period.) The most successful crop in the southern part of Carolina was rice, which the slaves had had experience growing in West Africa. In the more elevated, rockier terrain of the north, livestock, tobacco, and lumber produced a more balanced economy less dependent on slave labor. North and South Carolina split into separate colonies in 1701.

In 1733, **James Ogelthorpe** brought a group of debtors from England to found the colony of Georgia. Once again, proprietors sought to institute their idea of a utopian settlement, and once again the openness of conditions in America prevented that sort of regulation. The initial intention for Georgia was to ban slavery and alcohol while developing a planned community whose economy revolved around the cultivation and use of silkworms. None of these ideas fit the intentions of the settlers themselves. In 1750, the trustees abandoned their plan and left Georgia to develop much like its neighbor, South Carolina.

### The Settling of Pennsylvania

One of the more radical sects of Protestantism, Quakerism began in England in the mid-seventeenth century. Quakers believed that the spirit of God was expressed through an "inner light" within each believer, rather than through the tenets of an organized church. They considered the Church of England corrupt and refused to pay any taxes that might support it. They rejected any form of social hierarchy on the grounds that no social distinctions existed in the sight of God, and for the same reason they insisted on the spiritual equality of men and women. As deeply committed pacifists, they refused to participate in militia service. These beliefs and practices brought them mockery and persecution, exacerbated all the more by their energetic efforts to convert other Christian sects to their views.

In the mid-1660s, **William Penn**, a well-connected Englishman whose father was close to King Charles II, converted to Quakerism. Quakers looked to North America as the ideal place to further their cause, and in 1674 Penn was among a group of them establishing a settlement in West Jersey (western New Jersey). However, his dream was projected much farther in 1681 when he received a vast expanse of territory between Maryland and New York as his own proprietary colony, Pennsylvania.

Penn set about to structure his colony as a utopian "peaceable kingdom." He established religious freedom for Quakers, of course, but for all other religious persuasions as well. He was particularly concerned with achieving peaceful relations with the Indian tribes of his region and never sold any land without scrupulously buying it from them first.

Ironically, the success of Penn's policies became their undoing. Such was the appeal of Pennsylvania that it attracted large numbers of Scots-Irish and German immigrants who had little of Penn's concern about fairness to Indians, as well as new tribes of Indians themselves, moving there to avoid harsh relations with Whites elsewhere. By the mid-1700s, Pennsylvania was facing the same tensions over race and land that had beset other colonies. In a similar way, Penn's Quaker idealism eroded in other areas as well. But if pure Quakerism failed to direct the course of Pennsylvania in every respect, it remained a perceptible moral force within the colony, and later within the larger nation. The multiethnic settlement of Pennsylvania reflected a pattern found elsewhere in the Middle Atlantic colonies as well.

## The Great Awakening

From the 1730s to the 1760s, a wave of religious revivalism swept the colonies, beginning with the work of **Jonathan Edwards** in Massachusetts, then focusing on the evangelical efforts of **George Whitefield**. A former actor, Whitefield used those talents with great effect before large crowds as he traveled widely throughout the colonies, calling people back to orthodox Calvinism and a religious intensity that had faded since the preceding century. The fervor stirred up in the **Great Awakening** led to competition between different denominations, which in turn tended to weaken support for formally established religion and to encourage the separation of Church and State. Beyond its religious impact, the Great Awakening had significant influence on secular life in America. It brought women into a role of more direct participation, inspired the founding of several colleges, supported a more egalitarian social outlook, and drew people from isolated colonies together into their first broadly based American experience.

## British Imperial Policy for the Colonies

As soon as the Stuart family was restored to the throne in 1660, King Charles II turned his attention to the management of commerce between England and the colonies. Like other European rulers of his time, he was influenced by the theory of **mercantilism**, which viewed economic life as a direct competition for wealth against other nations. The nation considered most successful was the one that exported the most to others while having the least need to import from them. Colonies were an integral part of the strategy in this competition, both for their resources and as ready markets for the nation's own produce.

England enacted these mercantile policies in a series of three laws known as the **Navigation Acts**, which applied to all of her North American colonies. These laws specified the following:

- No goods could be sent to or taken from the colonies except in a British-owned ship with a British captain and a crew at least three-quarters British. (British included residents of British colonies.) Also, items on an "enumerated list," such as sugar, tobacco, cotton, and indigo, could only be exported to England or other British ports. (1660)

- Goods sent to the colonies from anywhere in Europe had to pass first through a British port where import and export duties could be levied. (1663)

- Goods leaving the colonies would be taxed as they left the port unless they were items on the enumerated list going directly to an English destination. Also, customs officials would be put in place to enforce these restrictions. (1673)

All English colonists were not affected equally by these laws. Those with a product very much in demand in England, such as tobacco, benefited from the mercantile monopoly on the market.

Those colonists who lived inland on largely self-sufficient farms were relatively unaffected. However, those living along the coast whose livelihoods depended upon trade and commerce found these laws quite confining, and they often resorted to smuggling to circumvent them.

In 1664, during the course of a naval war with the Dutch, England strengthened its North American empire by seizing the port of New Amsterdam and with it the entire New Netherlands colony. Though the Dutch briefly regained control of this territory in 1672, by 1673 it was firmly back in English hands, renamed New York for the king's brother, the Duke of York. In this same year, Parliament established the **Lords of Trade and Plantations**, a board to oversee colonial affairs. Feeling that Massachusetts needed to be brought into line even more, in 1679 the Lords of Trade overruled its claims to New Hampshire, making New Hampshire a separate royal colony. In 1684, the original charter for Massachusetts was revoked, and it was made a royal colony, too.

In 1686, after the death of Charles II, the former Duke of York, now James II, cracked down on New England even more. Connecticut, Rhode Island, Plymouth, Massachusetts Bay, New Hampshire, and shortly afterward New York and New Jersey were all combined to form the **Dominion of New England**, under the governorship of **Sir Edmund Andros**. All representative assemblies in these colonies were abolished, town meetings were forbidden, and the Navigation Acts were strictly enforced.

This trend toward stiff control was suddenly altered in 1688 with the **Glorious Revolution**, which toppled James II and the Stuart family from power. The Glorious Revolution was immediately echoed in Boston where Edmund Andros was ousted and sent back to England. The Dominion was disbanded and popular assemblies reinstated. Massachusetts, Plymouth, and the territory that is now Maine were incorporated as a single colony under a governor appointed by the Crown.

There was a similar response in New York, where the Dominion official was thrown out and his place taken by a German merchant named Jacob Leisler. However, Leisler himself fell victim to enemies among the English/Dutch elite of the city. Though no one mourned the passing of James II's control, Leisler was tried for treason and executed in 1691. **Leisler's Rebellion** revealed rifts in New York's economy and society that remained for decades.

The upheavals of authority in the years before and after the Glorious Revolution may have been a factor in the tension that erupted in 1692 with the **witchcraft trials in Salem, Massachusetts**. Within a short period of time, 100 citizens of the town were imprisoned on charges of witchcraft, and 19 were executed. The interweaving of superstition, family, and religious hatreds within the village and the broader anxieties over authority in the colony, all of which played themselves out in the witchcraft episode, will probably never be clearly understood.

William and Mary, England's new rulers, replaced the Lords of Trade and Plantations with a new **Board of Trade** to oversee the Navigation Acts. They also continued the Stuart trend toward consolidating colonies under royal control, with appointed governors who could veto any decision made by a representative assembly. In 1732, to protect British sugar growers in the West Indies, Parliament passed the **Molasses Act**, which put a tax on cheaper French molasses being imported into the colonies. New Englanders simply evaded the tax through smuggling or bribing customs officials. On the whole, however, William and Mary moved away from the Stuarts' attempts to bring the American colonies under tight control. For the next 50 years or more, the colonies entered a period of **salutary neglect**, during which they could work out their own fortunes with only minimal direction from England.

## The English and French Struggle for North America

England and France were at war more or less continuously from 1689 to 1713, and fighting then resumed in 1744. The fundamental issue in these wars was the control of trade, and battles were fought from India to North America. In the first wave of fighting, America was only a side theater of action. However, the second wave became in part a struggle for the possession of North America itself, focusing particularly on the western lands from the Ohio River valley up to the Great Lakes. The English had an advantage in the firmness of their settlements and the size of their American population. The French, on their side, often had more organized armies and could draw on far more support from the Indian tribes, with the crucial exception of the powerful **Iroquois League**.

The final phase of this conflict began in 1754 with the **Seven Years' War**, known in America as the **French and Indian War**. At a congress in Albany, New York, in June of that year, **Benjamin Franklin**, fearing the troubles to come, proposed a plan for uniting the colonies under a federal council, with representatives from each one and a presiding official appointed by the Crown. Despite the threat they all faced, the colonies felt no impulse whatsoever toward unity. To Franklin's disgust, not one of them approved the **Albany Plan of Union**.

Despite setbacks in the first years of the war, the English persisted. In 1759, English general **James Wolfe** defeated the French general **Louis Joseph, Marquis de Montcalm** for possession of Quebec, in a battle in which both men died. From this point on, it was clear that France had lost its American empire. The war took a few more years to end elsewhere in the world, but when the **Treaty of Paris** was signed in 1763, it ended the power of the French in North America.

# The Outbreak of the American Revolution
# (1763–1776)

In the wake of its victory over France, England turned toward her American colonies with a new outlook. Changing from recent decades of "salutary neglect," Parliament intended to take a firmer hand with patterns of settlement in America and sought to defray some of the expenses of the empire by raising tax revenues from the colonies. This policy brought resistance from some colonists.

England's first move was to establish the **Proclamation Line of 1763**, which forbade settlement west of the Allegheny Mountains, offering some protection to the Indians living there. This move was not unpopular with some colonists along the seacoast, for it promised to guard the populations and labor supply there from western migration. It was resented by that minority of poorer colonists willing to risk hardship and Indian attack for a fresh start in the west. A standing army of 10,000 men was established to enforce the Proclamation Line, to be supported at the colonists' expense.

In the following year, Parliament imposed the **Sugar Act**, a new tax on molasses, which was imported to New England from the West Indies to make rum. This tax was actually less than the previous rate, but unlike that prior tax, this one was strictly enforced, so that those who had previously avoided any payment through smuggling felt the pinch.

In 1765, Parliament passed the Stamp Act. All sorts of commonly used paper items, such as newspapers, playing cards, legal documents, and calendars had to be fixed with a government stamp for which a tax was paid. Funds from the tax were to be used to maintain a British army in America, a protection some felt less in need of after the defeat of the French. A comparable law had been in place in England for several years, but Americans were strongly opposed to it. Some reasoned that an **external tax** on imported luxury items would be less offensive than this **internal tax** on everyday items; others objected to taxation in more general terms.

Representatives from the different colonies met at the **Stamp Act Congress** to draft a formal protest to Parliament. A more immediate approach was taken by a group called the **Sons of Liberty**, who used noncompliance, propaganda, and acts of violence to intimidate officials from collecting the tax. **Nonimportation Agreements**, boycotts of British goods, were practiced throughout the colonies and brought pressure to bear on English merchants.

Parliament reacted by repealing the Stamp Act in 1766. However, it simultaneously passed the **Declaratory Act**, which proclaimed Parliament's right to pass laws for the colonies "in all cases whatsoever." British officials also began to issue **Writs of Assistance**, which permitted British officials to search colonial homes and warehouses for smuggled goods.

In 1767, Parliament passed a series of revenue bills known as the **Townshend Acts**. They included:

- a series of "external taxes" on various items imported;

- a provision that called for the salaries of colonial governors and judges to be paid out of the new revenues and not by colonial legislatures;

- the reorganization of the Customs Office to improve the enforcement of the various British taxes and regulations.

In addition, specific instructions were given to the British governor in New York to veto any measure the New York assembly might pass until it paid for the billeting of its British troops.

Although ill will toward England still simmered among some colonists, the Townshend Acts defused the situation, and passions subsided. However, in 1770, an incident took place when ten British troops guarding the Customhouse, part of a contingent that had arrived in Boston in 1768, were set upon by a number of Bostonians critical of their presence. Five colonists were killed in what **Samuel Adams**, a radical Boston propagandist, called **The Boston Massacre**. In a subsequent trial, John Adams, a respected leader in Boston, was the lawyer who defended the soldiers. A jury of colonists acquitted them. Meanwhile, John Adams's cousin Samuel wrote an account of the incident entitled "Innocent Blood Crying to God from the Streets of Boston."

Again, there was a lull in tensions. While that was an agreeable development to some colonists, others feared a loss of momentum to events. To increase communication throughout the various English colonies in North America, this group formed **Committees of Correspondence**, which encouraged colonial resistance to the British.

The **Boston Tea Party** occurred in 1773. Parliament had passed the **Tea Act** in an effort to bail out the financially troubled East India Company, a massive corporation facing bankruptcy with millions of pounds of tea in its warehouses. This gave the company a monopoly on colonial trade in the commodity and resulted in three things:

1.  the colonial tea drinker was able to purchase better tea at a cheaper price than before;

2.  colonial merchants and smugglers who had previously profited from the sale of tea lost money; and

3.  the precedent for further such trade monopolies was established.

In December, to protest the Tea Act, a group of Bostonians dressed as Indians descended on an East India ship at anchor and threw its cargo into the harbor. Similar "tea parties" took place in a number of colonial ports.

In retaliation for the tea parties, Parliament passed the **Coercive Acts** in 1774 (quickly termed the **Intolerable Acts** by the colonists). These closed Boston Harbor to all trade, removed the colonial assembly's power to appoint an advisory council for the royal governor, forbade town meetings, and required colonial homes to house British soldiers.

Also in 1774, Parliament passed the **Quebec Act**, which provided administration for the Canadian lands acquired from France by the Treaty of Paris in 1763. Quebec was given control over much of the land between the Ohio and Mississippi Rivers, at the expense of colonial claims. Protection was also given to the Roman Catholic Church and to French institutions and traditions in Canada; no representative assembly was projected for the new colony. Although Parliament had worked on this law for ten years, and although it was designed for Quebec's distinctive French culture, American colonists saw each of its provisions as a veiled attack on their own liberties.

In response to both the Intolerable Acts and the Quebec Act, the Massachusetts Assembly called for a **Continental Congress**, or gathering, which ultimately convened in Philadelphia in September of 1774. The Congress called for a boycott of English goods and passed John Adams's **Declaration of Rights and Grievances**. This declaration used the "natural law" philosophy of

John Locke and the Enlightenment as well as English legal precedent to argue that the colonies could be taxed only by their own representative assemblies. British legal authorities answered that under the practice of **Virtual Representation**, all English citizens were represented equally in Parliament, regardless of where in the empire they resided.

# The American Revolution (1776–1783)

Alarmed by the signs of colonial unrest, the British commander in Boston decided to confiscate supplies of firearms and gunpowder rumored to be stockpiled at Concord, 20 miles west of the city. Warned by Paul Revere and William Dawes, colonial "minutemen" gathered in a show of force on Lexington Green. Shots were fired (no one knows which side fired first), and several colonists were killed. The British forces proceeded to Concord. However, they were prevented from crossing the Concord River by assembled militias from a number of communities under the erroneous impression that the British had set fire to the town. During their retreat to Boston, the British troops suffered substantial losses, largely to colonial sharpshooters hiding behind trees and stone walls along the line of march.

Immediately following the Battle of Concord, a **Second Continental Congress** assembled in Philadelphia. This assembly, with no clear legal authority, remained in session throughout the revolution. Its first steps were to authorize a Colonial Army with Virginian **George Washington** as commander and to license colonial privateers to prey on British shipping.

In an attempt to force the British troops to abandon Boston, colonists under the cover of night seized Breeds' Hill across the harbor from Boston (next to Bunker Hill, where the colonists intended to be and which would have put them out of range of the British ships). The colonists were forced to retreat in the face of superior forces, but British losses were substantial. Soon thereafter, colonial forces were able to mount cannons captured at Fort Ticonderoga on the Dorchester Heights to the south of the city, placing the British fleet in jeopardy. British troops and colonial sympathizers were removed to Halifax, Nova Scotia, not to return to New England for the duration of the war.

The colonists' willingness to consider revolution was substantially increased by the publication of Thomas Paine's pamphlet, **Common Sense**, which argued persuasively that the colonies had no reasonable course but to sever themselves completely from Great Britain.

The **Declaration of Independence**, signed in July of 1776 by delegates to the Second Continental Congress, defended the action of the colonies by appeals to reason and natural law.

British commander William Howe decided to seize New York City as his headquarters and sailed from Halifax in the spring of 1776. George Washington attempted to defend the city but suffered serious losses at Brooklyn Heights and White Plains. Pursued across New Jersey, Washington did achieve an eventual victory by crossing the Delaware River on Christmas night, catching Hessian troops at Trenton unprepared after holiday celebrations. Soon thereafter, American troops also achieved victory at Princeton before going into winter quarters at Morristown, NJ.

In 1777, the British attempted to cut off New England, which they considered the most rebellious region, from the rest of the American colonies. They sent Gen. John Burgoyne south from Montreal along Lake Champlain and down the Hudson River, where he was to meet with Gen. Howe's troops marching north from New York. To complete the strategy, Col. St. Leger was ordered to proceed west up the St. Lawrence River into Lake Ontario and then to march east toward Albany. However, the plan failed when St. Leger's forces were pushed back by colonial troops under Benedict Arnold, and Burgoyne, weighted down with excess equipment and unaware of the difficulties to be faced in penetrating the New England forests, was forced to surrender his entire force at Saratoga.

Howe's forces never went north. Instead, he determined to seize another major colonial city, Philadelphia, and he sailed into Chesapeake Bay in the fall of 1777. Washington's forces made several unsuccessful attempts to stop him, first at **Brandywine**, then at Germantown just outside the city. While Howe's forces were made welcome in Philadelphia, Washington's forces spent a humiliating and uncomfortable winter at **Valley Forge**.

One sign of light was that in March of 1778, encouraged by the American victory at Saratoga, France signed a treaty of alliance with the new United States, providing the country with increased money and supplies and, perhaps more importantly, greatly increasing American morale. A year later, Spain also took up arms against Great Britain. At this point, British authorities decided to concentrate on pacifying the southern states, convinced that there Loyalist support would be at its height. Successful in taking Savannah (December 1778) and Charleston (May 1780), the British forces still found themselves subject to hit-and-run attacks. At King's Mountain, SC in October of 1780, American troops defeated a large band of **Tories**. Battles at both Cowpens, SC and Guilford Court House, NC were costly for the British forces under **Gen. Cornwallis**. Cornwallis was then ordered to retreat to Yorktown, Virginia, to await a British fleet sent to evacuate his troops.

However, Cornwallis found himself in an untenable position after the arrival of a French fleet from the West Indies and a forced march by a combined French/American force from New York under Washington and French Commander Count de **Rochambeau**. Thus, on October 19, 1781, Cornwallis surrendered his entire force.

The **Treaty of Paris of 1783** officially ended the war. The boundaries of the United States were set at Canada to the north, Florida to the south, and the Mississippi River to the west. Great Britain agreed to abandon its fur trading forts in American territory, and in exchange the United States agreed to pay legitimate debts owed English merchants and to encourage individual states to restore property and rights to American Loyalists who had fled the states during the revolution.

# The Era of the Articles of Confederation (1783–1789)

The **Articles of Confederation** were written by delegates to the Second Continental Congress in 1777, but ratification did not come immediately.  A major issue dividing many of the states was the status of American lands west of the Allegheny Mountains.  States without claims to these lands feared they would be at a disadvantage if revenue from land sales went to individual states rather than to the nation as a whole.  New York and Connecticut yielded their claims in 1780, and Virginia finally agreed to do the same in 1781.  The Articles remained in force until the ratification of the **Constitution** in 1788.  (Note:  From 1777 until 1781, the Continental Congress had operated without any clear legal sanction.)

The structure of the government created by the Articles of Confederation included:

- a unicameral (single chamber) legislature with each state having a single vote, regardless of its relative population (although each state could have between 5 and 13 delegates to Congress);

- no provision for a president or executive officer;

- the requirement for a two-thirds majority to pass any major legislation, and unanimous approval to alter the Articles themselves;

- no provision for a national judicial system.

Certain powers were given to the national government.  It could:

- make war or peace with other nations;

- determine relative state populations in order to determine each state's quota of soldiers and taxes;

- admit new states and settle interstate disputes;

- establish post offices, coinage, and standard weights and measure.

However, it could not:

- raise its own army; it could merely request the use of the various state militias;

- directly tax individual citizens or institutions; it could only request from a particular state an amount of money determined by that state's relative population.  How that money was raised was up to the individual state;

- regulate interstate trade.

Faced with the problem of administering the western lands ceded to it by the various states, the Articles government passed the **Land Ordinance of 1785**, which provided for the land to be surveyed and divided into townships, reserving certain lots for schools and civic buildings and offering the rest for sale.

The years of the Revolution were boom times for farmers, since both American and British troops needed food.  Many farmers went deep into debt during these years to expand their farms.  However, after the war ended, the demand for food slackened, and many farmers found themselves in trouble.  In 1784, in Worcester County, Massachusetts, alone, 2,000 lawsuits were filed for debt.

The situation worsened when many creditors, distrusting the paper money in circulation, began to demand only gold or silver for repayment of debt. A western Massachusetts farmer and a former captain in the revolutionary army, **Daniel Shays**, led a rebellion in 1786, refusing to permit further foreclosures on farms and demanding that large quantities of paper money be printed and tax relief be offered farmers. The rebellion was eventually put down, but some felt that the states, by themselves, were unable to deal effectively with such revolts.

The new nation also experienced difficulties on the international scene. Foreign nations found that the new national government often didn't have the power to compel individual states to accept its decisions. As a result, such nations often preferred to deal directly with state officials. In addition, the newly formed country did not have the strength to protect her vital interests. One indication of this came in 1784 when Spain closed the lower part of the Mississippi to American shipping.

In 1787, Congress passed the **Northwest Ordinance of 1787**, which outlined the various steps to be taken by the territories in the Northwest on their way to statehood. The ordinance set specific population levels that had to be met at each stage, mandated religious freedom in the territories, and forbade the institution of slavery.

During the fall of 1786, delegates from five states met in a convention in Annapolis, Maryland, (the **Annapolis Convention**) to discuss altering the Articles. They were concerned about their states' economic difficulties, which they blamed on the inability of the national government to regulate interstate trade. Led by **Alexander Hamilton** of New York, these delegates called for another convention to meet in Philadelphia in the spring of 1787. At this second convention, it was quickly acknowledged that merely revising the Articles of Confederation would not correct the problems many attending the convention felt faced the country. Therefore, without specific authorization, the delegates undertook to create a new form of government. Instead of a "Confederation" of separate sovereign states cooperating in specific areas, such as national defense, they opted for a system in which the states give up certain rights and powers to a strong central government. This decision was by no means universally popular, either among the delegates to the Philadelphia convention or among the country as a whole.

To achieve their goal, the delegates were compelled to reach several compromises among themselves.

- The **Great Compromise** (also known as the "Connecticut Compromise"): Smaller states favored a legislative structure similar to the Articles wherein each state, regardless of population, is represented equally; larger states felt that their relative size should be taken into consideration. The solution: A bicameral (two-house) system wherein each state receives two delegates in the Senate and a number of delegates reflecting the state's relative population in the House of Representatives. For a proposal to become law, it has to pass both houses in identical form.

- The **Three-Fifths Compromise**: Slave states wanted all slaves counted as population for the purpose of determining the number of delegates a state had in the House of Representatives but not for the purpose of determining the state's tax quota. The solution: Three-fifths of the slaves would be counted for both purposes.

- The **Commerce Compromise**: Southern states, heavily dependent on European markets for their produce, were unwilling to grant the national government the power to tax such exports; many northerners felt the new government should have the right to regulate both interstate and international trade. The solution: Congress could regulate interstate trade and could place tariffs on imports but not exports.

Delegates at the convention wrestled with the issue of slavery itself, but those in favor of abolishing it met with no success. In the final version of the Constitution, the word "slavery" was never mentioned; however, the existence of the institution was acknowledged with the tacit acceptance of certain clauses. The African slave trade was given limited protection by a provision forbidding the national government from interfering with the "Importation of such Persons as any of the States . . . shall think proper to admit" until 1808. (The federal government did indeed outlaw the importation of slaves in 1808, but by that time the native population of slave was more than enough to support an active slave trade in the South.)

To ratify the Constitution, the delegates decided not to rely on state legislatures. They felt that if state legislatures gave initial approval to the Constitution, they might, in the future, feel they could take it away. Instead, the delegates agreed on the creation of special state conventions exclusively for the purpose of ratification.

The ratification of the Constitution was by no means a foregone conclusion. Several states made it a condition of ratification that a **Bill of Rights** be amended to the Constitution immediately after ratification to further protect individual freedoms. This was agreed to.

The proposed Constitution encountered considerable opposition in some quarters from those called the **Anti-Federalists**. Though this group included a variety of opinions, their concerns converged on the fears that individual states would lose their autonomy to a powerful central government and that corruption of that central government's power could move back in the direction of monarchy.

When the time came to vote, the new Constitution won by comfortable margins in most states, though Anti-Federalist sentiment was particularly well-organized in the crucial state of New york. To persuade voters here, Alexander Hamilton, James Madison, and John Jay wrote the ***Federalist Papers***, a series of articles supporting various aspects of the new government. The most famous of these essays, Madison's **Federalist #10**, argues that the national government will offer safe defense of property from the passions of political factions. In a close vote, New York gave its approval, and the new government came into being.

# The Federalist Period
# (1789–1800)

The **electoral college** (a group established under the Constitution and charged with the responsibility of making the actual selection) unanimously elected George Washington president. He developed the concept of a **cabinet** to advise him. The first cabinet included Alexander Hamilton as Secretary of Treasury and **Thomas Jefferson** as Secretary of State (in charge of the nation's foreign affairs).

The new Congress passed several pieces of legislation, including the Tariff of 1789, which provided for the national government's main source of income through a moderate tax on certain imported items, and the Judiciary Act of 1789, which fleshed out the federal court system, consisting of the Supreme Court, three circuit courts, and one district court per state. The country continued its reliance on the common law traditions of England wherein decisions of previous courts (precedents) are used as guides by current courts.

In 1791, the nation took the first step toward expansion when Vermont became the 14th state.

During Washington's first administration, Alexander Hamilton set before Congress a series of recommendations for the country's economic policies. In each case, Hamilton encountered opposition, led by Thomas Jefferson and James Madison, then Speaker of the House of Representatives. Soon two political parties crystallized: the **Federalists** (Hamilton and those agreeing with him) and the **Republicans** (or "Antifederalists:" Jefferson, Madison, and their followers). Hamilton's proposals can be grouped into three categories:

## The Report of Public Credit

The Issue:

> During the revolution, both the national government and the individual states had borrowed large amounts of money, by selling bonds, to finance the war. The national government owed $54 million both to foreign investors, mostly French and Dutch, and to individual Americans. Various states owed an additional $20 million. Some argued that since the Articles of Confederation government had, in effect, been overthrown, the new national government had no obligation to repay these debts.

Hamilton's Proposal:

> In order to establish strong financial credibility, the federal government should both fund the existing national government debt by borrowing money from citizens and assume (take over) all debts contracted during the war by individual states, thus guaranteeing their eventual repayment.

The Reaction:

> Most agreed that debts to foreigners should be repaid. There was less agreement as to that portion owed to Americans since, in many cases, these bonds were no longer owned by the original purchaser, but by speculators (some of the friends of Hamilton) who had bought them at a substantial discount, and who thus stood to make a huge profit. In addition, some states, most notably Georgia and Virginia, had already paid off their debts and objected strongly to assuming the debts of other states.

The Result:

> Despite Madison's objections, Congress adopted Hamilton's policies concerning the funding of the national debt. Madison finally agreed to the assumption of the state debts in return for an agreement moving the nation's capitol to the newly created District of Columbia, adjacent to Virginia.

## The Report on a National Bank

The Issue:

> Hamilton proposed the establishment of a national bank (20 percent of which was to be funded by the national government, 80 percent by private investors) that could be operated throughout all the states. He argued that such a bank, in addition to serving as a repository for national funds, could collect taxes, provide a stable and trusted paper currency, and stimulate business growth through loans.

The Reaction:

> Business and commercial interests were in favor of the bank; farmers and those in debt were afraid that such a bank, controlling the supply of currency available in the economy, would curtail inflation, which was helping them. Madison and Jefferson argued that such a bank was beyond the legitimate scope of the national government since the Constitution nowhere specifically grants the national government the ability to create such a bank (this became known as the **Strict Constructionist** approach to the Constitution). Hamilton, on the other hand, argued that the Constitution contained an "implied power" for such an institution (**Broad** or **Loose Construction**).

The Result:

> The proposal passed the Congress. In the House of Representatives, the vote was 39–20. Thirty-six of the affirmative votes came from the Northern states; 19 of the opposing votes came from the South. Washington had some doubts about the bank's constitutionality but let the measure pass.

## The Report on Manufactures

The Issue:

> Hamilton wanted to encourage the growth of manufacturing within the United States, both to increase employment and to provide a greater degree of self-sufficiency in case of war. He proposed that the country's **infant industries** be protected from European competition, especially British, by means of a high **protective tariff** on foreign imports.

The Reaction:

> Obviously, owners and workers at these infant industries were in favor. Those opposed included farmers, who had to import much of their equipment; consumers in general, who found their cost of living thus increased; and coastal merchants involved in international trade.

The Result:

> The Tariff Act of 1792 increased levels somewhat, though not to the level sought by Hamilton. (**Note on Tariffs**: With his report on manufactures, Hamilton introduced the ongoing and often divisive issue of tariffs into American politics. As the reaction in 1792 indicated, tariffs were generally supported by those with a close connection to industrial growth and opposed by those who saw themselves as separate from industrial interests. Until the mid-

nineteenth century, tariff disputes had a strong regional aspect, since industrial growth was then taking place primarily in the northeast. The regional element became less distinct as industry spread beyond that area. Tariff issues remained prominent through the 1930s. In the post-World War II years, a heightened interest in promoting foreign trade caused the issue to recede. While the monetary details of tariffs are not discussed here, the tariffs themselves as they occur from the 1790s to the 1930s are worth attention, for they give one of the clearest indications of which groups are exerting political power at a given time.)

A major technological development occurred in 1793 when inventor **Eli Whitney** perfected the **cotton gin**. By permitting the rapid separation of cottonseeds from cotton, this device created an enormous new export crop for southern farmers. Whitney also played an important role in manufacturing by developing the concept of interchangeable parts for machines.

An important issue dividing Federalists and Republicans was the French Revolution, which broke out in 1789, and the subsequent conflict between France and Great Britain. Federalists tended to side with Britain; Republicans were more sympathetic with the goals of the Revolution. In 1793, **Citizen Genêt** was sent to the United States to stir up support for France's war against Great Britain and to encourage American expeditions against British ally Spain in Florida and Louisiana. However, Washington issued a **Proclamation of Neutrality**, and Citizen Genêt was relieved of his position by the French government.

In 1794, the national government faced another threat when farmers in western Pennsylvania rebelled against an excise tax that had been placed on whiskey. The farmers were accustomed to converting their grain into whiskey so that it could be easily transported over the Allegheny Mountains, and they resented both the tax and the procedures of search and seizure and trial that were utilized to collect it. However, 13,000 militiamen called out by Washington quickly put down the rebellion. Washington thus set a significant precedent by using the power of the new government to suppress a rebellious group of its own citizens.

The new government devoted much attention to establishing working relationships with other nations. In 1795, three treaties were signed.

**Jay's Treaty** (with England):
> England had not abandoned its forts in the Northwest as agreed in the Treaty of Paris (1783) and was thought to be encouraging Indian unrest in the region. England, for her part, argued that the U.S. had failed to honor its obligations under the same treaty to the Loyalists and British merchants. In addition, British ships, at war with France, were seizing American ships trading with the French West Indies and were also boarding American ships to seize sailors whom the British claimed were deserters from British ships (**impressment**). The treaty secured British withdrawal from the Northwest forts but failed to settle the maritime issues. It was received unenthusiastically in the Senate and barely ratified. The British practice of impressment continued.

**Pickney's Treaty** (with Spain; a.k.a. The Treaty of San Lorenzo):
> Spain agreed to open the Mississippi "in its whole length from its source to the ocean" to American shipping, permitted American use of the port of New Orleans for three years, and clarified the northern border of Florida.

**The Treaty of Greenville** (with Indians of the Northwest):

In 1794, Gen. "Mad Anthony" Wayne defeated the Indians of the Northwest at the Battle of Fallen Timbers.  In 1795, the Indians agreed to abandon most of the Northwest to white settlement.

Washington's **Farewell Address** in 1796 (largely written by Hamilton) carried within it several significant points:

- It established the tradition of a president serving no more than two terms (not broken until Franklin Roosevelt in 1940).

- It warned that the U.S. was still an experiment in Republican government, and warned against "partisanship."

- It expressed dismay at growing sectionalism and its dangers.

- It suggested that in foreign affairs, the United States should "avoid foreign entanglements."

Washington's vice president, John Adams, was elected the nation's second president.  He faced an immediate crisis with France, which, feeling the United States was too sympathetic to England (Jay's Treaty), had begun to harass American shipping and refused to recognize a new American ambassador.  Adams sent a delegation of three men to improve relations, but the French foreign minister, M. Talleyrand, refused even to meet with them unless the United States apologized for remarks made by Adams, loaned France $10 million, and paid a $250,000 bribe to Talleyrand himself.  The United States government was incensed, a feeling shared by most Americans.  ("Millions for defense, but not one cent for tribute!" was the cry.)  This became known as the **XYZ Affair**, since the French agents were so designated in official reports.  Congress approved funding to increase the navy and repealed all treaties with France.  For several years (1798-1799), an undeclared naval war took place in the West Indies between the two countries.

Federalists in Congress proclaimed their fears about the growing number of immigrants, allegedly unfamiliar with the American political system and therefore unprepared to immediately fulfill the responsibilities of citizenship.  In 1798, they passed a series of measures known as the **Alien and Sedition Acts**.

- The Naturalization Act extended the time required before an immigrant could apply for citizenship from 5 to 14 years.

- The Alien Act empowered the president to deport any alien considered to be dangerous and, in time of war, to arrest all aliens from the hostile nation.

- The Sedition Act established heavy fines and possible jail sentences for those "conspiring to oppose" the laws or "publishing false, scandalous . . . writings" against the president, Congress, or the government in general.

Adams did not promote these bills; nor did he veto them.  Ten Republican editors and writers were convicted under the terms of the Sedition Act; many others were charged but acquitted.  No Federalists were charged under the law.

In response to the Alien and Sedition Acts, the legislatures of Virginia and Kentucky set forth declarations known as the **Virginia and Kentucky Resolutions**.  The Virginia Resolution (written by Madison) claimed that each state had the right to make the final determination as to the constitutionality of measures passed by Congress. The Kentucky Resolution (by Jefferson) went further by claiming that a state had the right to declare invalid ("nullify") an act of Congress considered by that state to be unconstitutional.

In the **election of 1800**, Republicans Thomas Jefferson and Aaron Burr defeated Adams. Under the rules of the day, each member of the electoral college voted for two men; the one receiving the highest number of votes became the president, the next highest became the vice president. The Republicans had planned that one elector would not vote for Burr, thus guaranteeing Jefferson the highest number of votes. Somehow this plan didn't work, and as a result both Jefferson and Burr ended up with the same number of votes, thus throwing the election into the House of Representatives. Here, Hamilton was able to throw the election to Jefferson after receiving assurances that Jefferson wouldn't completely sweep away Federalist programs. (Jefferson referred to this election and the transfer of power from the Federalists to the Republicans as the **Revolution of 1800**.) After the Jefferson/Burr confusion, the Twelfth Amendment was passed, mandating that voting in the electoral college specify president and vice president.

# The Jeffersonian Era Through the War of 1812 (1800–1815)

As president, Jefferson abandoned a Federalist program to build 25 frigates for the navy, relying instead on a larger number of small, inexpensive gunboats useful primarily to defend the coast. In addition, he repealed an excise tax, but maintained the tariff and the national bank. He also repealed the Naturalization Act. Although he did not repeal the Alien or the Sedition Act, he allowed them to expire on their own without using or renewing them.

One of the most important episodes of Jefferson's presidency was the purchase of the **Louisiana Territory**. By 1803, in a secret treaty, France under Napoleon had regained the vast landholdings of the Mississippi that it had earlier yielded to Spain in the Treaty of Paris of 1763. Napoleon hoped to use this territory as the start of an expanded French empire. However, after experiencing unexpected difficulty in reconquering the island of Santo Domingo and realizing that he needed funds for his various European wars, Napoleon decided to abandon these plans. When envoys from Jefferson arrived in France, seeking to buy or rent land in New Orleans for use by American shippers, Napoleon instead offered to sell the entire Louisiana Territory. Jefferson had grave doubts about his constitutional authority to make such a purchase, but he ultimately agreed to the deal. Congress, after long and bitter debate, approved the treaty of sale. Even before the treaty had become final, Jefferson sent explorers **Lewis and Clark** to survey the area.

To many northern Federalists, the Louisiana Purchase represented a potential new state that would shift the balance of power to the west. Some went so far as to suggest that the northeastern states secede from the Union. Hamilton refused to support this plan, so they turned to Aaron Burr, who would be in a strategic position to help if he won the governorship of New York. However, he lost the election, in part due to Hamilton's opposition, and the Federalist plan faded. Soon after this loss, Burr challenged Hamilton to a duel and killed him. Burr then got involved in a somewhat confused scheme involving the Louisiana Territory. Jefferson had him arrested and tried for treason. However, Chief Justice John Marshall, reading literally the part of the Constitution requiring testimony from at least two witnesses to the same "overt action" in a treason case, acquitted him. The case was one of the first establishing the Supreme Court as the protector of the nation's civil liberties.

The Supreme Court also made history in its decision in the case of ***Marbury v. Madison*** (1803). During his last few weeks in office, anticipating the takeover of Jefferson and the Republicans, President John Adams appointed a number of federal judges—the so-called **midnight appointments**. Many of these new judges had already taken over their duties when Jefferson was sworn in, but in several cases the actual warrant (or official document certifying the appointment) hadn't been delivered, and Jefferson refused to hand the warrants over. William Marbury, who had been appointed to a judgeship, sued the government for his position and the case appeared before the Supreme Court with Chief Justice **John Marshall**.

Marshall, a Federalist, wanted both to embarrass Jefferson and to increase the powers and prestige of the Supreme Court. His final decision was complex indeed. On the one hand, Marshall ruled that Jefferson had exceeded his authority in refusing to issue the warrant. On the other hand, he ruled that even so, the Supreme Court was prevented from doing anything about it. The Constitution limited the Court to "appellate jurisdiction" (meaning it could only decide cases appealed to it from other courts), in all but a few clearly stated situations. The Judiciary Act of 1789 had expanded the range of "original jurisdiction," so the Supreme Court could seemingly pass judgment in the Marbury case. However, Marshall declared that the Judiciary Act was unconstitutional for having done so. Marbury lost his commission, but that was unimportant. Marshall's great victory was to secure for the Supreme Court the precedent of passing judgment on a law's constitutionality, known as **judicial review**, which refutes the Virginia and Kentucky Resolutions. Since he wasn't ordered by the court to do anything specific, Jefferson had nothing tangible to defy. He could only stand by and watch Marshall carry off this very important coup.

Faced with the fact that many federal judges were Federalists and by terms of the Constitution held office for life, Jefferson and his supporters attempted to use the power of impeachment to remove those with whom they disagreed. After some success against lower-court judges, they attempted to impeach Supreme Court Justice Samuel Chase, an outspoken Federalist. However, the Republican-dominated Senate, presided over by Aaron Burr, acquitted him, and the use of impeachment for political purposes was abandoned.

Foreign affairs continued to concern President Jefferson. One problem involved the **Barbary Pirates** off the northern coast of Africa. As with most European nations, the United States was accustomed to paying tribute to forestall attack. However, in 1801, the Tripoli pirates, feeling the tribute not high enough, began seizing American ships. Jefferson sent units of the American navy to the Mediterranean, and 1805 had restored peace to the area.

Although the pirate trouble was resolved, the British practice of impressment continued. In 1807, a U.S. ship, the ***Chesapeake***, was fired upon and then boarded by a British ship searching for "deserters." Jefferson demanded that the British apologize for the incident and cease the practice of impressment. Britain was willing to do the first but not the second. In addition, Napoleon attempted to blockade the coast of Europe to cut off all British trade, and in a series of decrees (the **Berlin Decree** (1806) and the **Milan Decree** (1807)) proclaimed that any ship trading with Britain would be subject to seizure by the French. The British responded in 1807 with their **Orders in Council**, which threatened the same to ships trading with the continent. Jefferson, seeking to avoid war with either France or Great Britain, sought to coerce both nations to respect American maritime rights by economic means. The **Embargo Act of 1807** forbade any American ship to sail to any foreign port. This act was very unpopular in the United States, idling as it did the entire American merchant fleet. In 1809, Congress repealed the Embargo Act and replaced it with the **Nonintercourse Act**, which merely forbade trade with France and Britain.

In 1809, **James Madison** replaced Jefferson as president. In 1810, in an attempt to satisfy American shippers hurt by the Nonintercourse Act, Congress passed **Macon's Bill #2**. This opened all of Europe to American merchants, but provided that if either France or Great Britain was to agree to respect American rights on the seas, the president could reimpose the embargo on the other. Napoleon did agree (in bad faith), and Madison cut off trade with Britain, which continued its practice of impressment.

The congressional election of 1810 brought to office a group of congressmen who became known as the **War Hawks**. Many of them were from the frontier, and they actively espoused a war with England. **Henry Clay** of Kentucky and **John C. Calhoun** of South Carolina were prominent among these. Not only did these men feel that national honor and pride demanded a war, but they also felt that such a war might well end with Canada in their possession.

Those from the frontier felt that a war with England might solve the continuing Indian problem. Led by Shawnee Chief **Tecumseh**, tribes from Florida to the upper Missouri had banded together to oppose further white expansion into lands guaranteed to the Indians by treaty. In 1811, **Gov. William Henry Harrison** was able to inflict a serious defeat on Tecumseh's forces at the **Battle of Tippecanoe** (fought while Tecumseh himself was absent). This was the largest massing of tribes ever to fight against the United States, and their defeat marked the end of significant Indian resistance in the Northwest. However, frontiersmen were convinced that as long as British traders in Canada supplied Indians with firearms, danger would remain.

In 1812, Madison finally asked Congress for a declaration of war against Great Britain, stressing the issues of impressment and the Orders in Council. The measure passed despite New York's and most of New England's opposition to the war.

Madison called for the creation of a 50,000 man national militia to fight the war. In six months, only 5,000 men joined up. In general, the country's military forces were ill prepared to fight anyone, much less powerful Great Britain. Attempts in 1812 to invade Canada at Detroit and Niagara were both unsuccessful. American naval forces met with some initial success, but the end of the war found them bottled up in their ports. American privateers did have success preying on British shipping.

In 1813, American forces under **Capt. Oliver Perry** defeated British naval forces on Lake Erie, permitting Gen. Harrison to raid Toronto and burn the Parliament buildings. However, with the abdication of Napoleon in 1814, Britain was able to concentrate her attention on North America. In August, to avenge the burning of Toronto, a British force invaded Washington, DC. and burned the Capitol building and the White House. However, they were unsuccessful in an attempt to capture Fort McHenry near Baltimore. (During this attack, **Francis Scott Key** wrote "The Star Spangled Banner," which later became the national anthem.) Another British force invaded the northern United States from Montreal but was defeated at Plattsburgh Bay in northern New York.

The war continued to be unpopular in New England, the region most seriously affected economically by the loss of British trade and by the blockade placed on American ports by the British fleet. In 1814, representatives from five New England states met at Hartford (the **Hartford Convention**). They sent a delegation to Washington with a report calling for certain changes in the Constitution, including limiting a president to a single term, prohibiting successive presidents from the same state (aimed at the **Virginia Dynasty**: Washington, Jefferson, Madison, and later Monroe), eliminating the Three-Fifths Compromise, and supporting the concept of nullification. However, by the time the delegation arrived in Washington early in 1815, news of **Andrew Jackson's** victory at New Orleans had arrived, a wave of patriotic feeling was sweeping the capital, and the New Englanders never formally delivered their report.

Jackson's successful defense of New Orleans actually took place after the Treaty of Ghent (1814), which ended the war, had been signed (but before news of the treaty had reached the United States). The war solved none of the issues dividing the two countries; it merely provided for a return to the status of affairs before the war. However, it did reassert the United States' independence of Great Britain and encourage the growth of American industries as manufacturers sprang up to supply consumers with goods usually imported from Britain. Also, as American workers found fewer jobs in the shipping industries, it resulted in an increase in western migration.

# The "Era of Good Feelings" (1815–1824)

The expression "Era of Good Feelings" has been applied to the years immediately following the War of 1812, a period in which two-party strife subsided and the Republicans controlled the government. The remnants of the Federalist Party were tarred by their involvement with the Hartford Convention, and the party essentially dissolved in 1817. However, the Republicans, with no common enemy to confront, were unable to retain their own cohesiveness.

The Northeast emerged from the war with a new interest in manufacturing. In 1813, Francis Cabot Lowell formed the Boston Manufacturing Company and, building upon the British example, he and his associates quickly extended the **Waltham System** of large-scale factory production to new areas of Massachusetts.

In 1815, President Madison sent to Congress a set of proposals that Henry Clay termed the **American System**. Included in these were the following:

- funding for a strong national defense, including new frigates for the navy, a standing army, and federal control over the state militias;

- a protective tariff, designed largely to protect industries;

- federal funds for roads and canals (internal improvements);

- the establishment of a **Second National Bank** (the first having expired in 1811).

Madison wanted these proposals to be considered as a package, since they were intended to offer something to each section of the country. However, this didn't happen. In 1816, two parts of the program passed Congress: the charter for the Second National Bank and the Tariff of 1816, an openly protective bill. The passage of the tariff was in part a reaction to Britain's decision to dump goods on the American market, even below cost, in an attempt to drive infant American industries out of business.

However, Madison then vetoed the **Bonus Bill** sponsored by John Calhoun, which provided funds to build roads and canals in the south, because he had come to feel that it was unconstitutional for the national government to spend money for projects wholly within a single state. As a result, the wealthier northern states were able to finance roads, canals, and later railroads, and did so, connecting these states to the states of the west. The poorer south remained increasingly isolated from both regions.

On the international scene, in 1817, the United States and Great Britain signed the **Rush-Bagot Agreement**, which provided that neither country would fortify the Great Lakes region, a principle eventually (1872) applied to the entire border between the U.S. and Canada. After James Monroe was elected president in 1818, the U.S. and Spain signed the **Adams-Onis Treaty** (1819) wherein Spain gave up her claims to Florida. The year before the signing of this treaty, Andrew Jackson had invaded northern Florida in pursuit of Indian parties that had raided Georgia. While he was there, Jackson seized two Spanish strongholds and executed two Englishmen whom he had accused of supplying the Indians with arms. After hesitating and consulting his cabinet, especially Secretary of State **John Quincy Adams**, President Monroe demanded that Spain either control the Indians or sell Florida to the United States. Spain sold Florida. (The Adams-Onis Treaty also set a boundary between Spanish territory and any territory the United States might subsequently acquire all the way to the Pacific Ocean. It is therefore sometimes called the **Transcontinental Treaty**.)

1819 saw a series of decisions by Marshall's Supreme Court that had a substantial impact on the federal structure of the United States. In ***Dartmouth College v. Woodward***, the Court prohibited New Hampshire from modifying the charter that established Dartmouth College. Not only did this protect contracts, including those establishing corporations, from state manipulation, but it also confirmed the Supreme Court as the final arbiter of many state conflicts. More important was the decision in the case of ***McCulloch v. Maryland***. The state of Maryland, attempting to defend its own banking industry, placed a tax on out-of-state banks doing business within the state; the Second National Bank was the only such institution. When the national government complained that a state could not tax an institution of the national government ("the power to tax involves the power to destroy"), the state responded that the National Bank itself was unconstitutional, since creating it was not a power granted by the Constitution to the national government. Using the theory of the "Broad Construction" of the Constitution, Marshall determined that the national government had a broad range of "implied powers" and that the phrase in the Constitution limiting acts of Congress to those "necessary and proper" for carrying out certain specified responsibilities should not be read literally. The result was that the national government gained substantial power in areas heretofore reserved to the states.

Tensions among the various sections of the country surfaced again when Missouri, a slave territory, applied for statehood. At that time, there was a balance in the Senate between slave and free states. Issues such as tariff levels, the National Bank, and internal improvements all had sectional overtones, so everyone was sensitive to the dangers of an imbalance. Henry Clay ultimately devised the **Missouri Compromise**, whereby the territory of Maine was separated from Massachusetts and granted statehood at the same time as Missouri, which came in as a slave state. In addition, the southern border of Missouri (latitude 36°30') was extended across the Louisiana Territory with the understanding that further slavery would be restricted to lands south of that line.

The Supreme Court considered whether an individual state could pass laws affecting interstate trade in the case of ***Gibbons v. Ogden*** (1824), which dealt with a New York law granting a steamship monopoly on the Hudson River. The Court decided that only the national government had such authority.

With the fall of Napoleon, conservative European leaders organized into the **Quadruple Alliance**. They were determined to return conditions to the way they had been before the revolutionary age broke out. One of their goals was to return much of Central and South America to the control of Spain; many of these areas had declared their independence during the confusion of the Napoleonic Wars. To forestall any such attempt, in 1824 Monroe issued a declaration that became known as the **Monroe Doctrine**, though it was largely the work of John Quincy Adams. In it he declared that:

- the Western Hemisphere was no longer open to colonization;
- any attempt to undermine existing governments in the hemisphere would be regarded as a hostile act toward the United States;
- the United States would not intervene in European affairs and expected European nations to avoid involvement in the American hemisphere.

It should be noted that the United States itself had very little ability to back up these brave words. However, Great Britain, in its own interest, was also determined to prevent the restoration of the Spanish Empire, and the British navy was a powerful dissuader.

# John Quincy Adams and the Jacksonian Era (1824–1840)

When it came time for the **election of 1824**, there was no formal opposition to the Republican Party, but the party had no single leader either. The result was confusion and fragmentation, with sectionalism coming to the fore. The frontrunners were Andrew Jackson from Tennessee and John Quincy Adams from Massachusetts, with Henry Clay and John C. Calhoun also in the race. While Jackson ended up with more votes than any other candidate, he failed to receive the majority of votes in the electoral college required by the Constitution for election. Therefore, the House of Representatives had to decide among the three candidates receiving the highest number of votes (Jackson, Adams, and Calhoun, in that order). Henry Clay, eliminated from consideration, had substantial influence in the House of Representatives where he served as Speaker, and he swung his support to Adams who, after his election, appointed Clay his Secretary of State. Jackson's supporters cried that a **corrupt bargain** had been struck between the two men.

Adams's programs were nationalistic in temper, featuring money for a strong navy, new roads, and the establishment of national colleges. The movement toward new forms of transportation was typified by the opening of the Erie Canal in 1825, linking Lake Erie in the west with the Hudson River in the east. However, Jackson's supporters in Congress blocked passage of most of Adams's proposals. To distinguish between the two groups, Adams's supporters began to call themselves the "National Republicans" while Jackson's group called itself the "Democratic Republicans," later shortened to "Democrats."

(**Note on American political parties**: America has had a consistent two-party tradition since the ratification of the Constitution. Broadly speaking, one party has tended to represent upper-middle-class propertied interests, the other supporting the "common man," although specific policies might shift and/or overlap at any given time. Party name shifts during the years before the Civil War can be confusing. Beginning with Jefferson, the party associated with the common man has been called the Republicans, then the Democratic Republicans, then the Democrats. The business-oriented party was less consistent in its membership, but it can be traced from the Federalists, to the National Republicans, to the Whig Party of the 1840s, and finally to the Republican Party founded in the early 1850s.)

In 1828, as thoughts turned to the coming presidential election, Congress passed the Tariff of 1828. It quickly became known as the **Tariff of Abominations**, which raised the level of tariffs to a new high. This appears to have been passed with the expectation that Adams would have to veto it because its rates were so steep, which would cost Adams northern support. However, he signed it, and the South reacted with shock.

In several ways, the **election of 1828** can be regarded as the first modern election. Since 1816, many property qualifications on the right to vote had been removed, first in frontier states, then in older states. Written ballots, which were easier to use, were introduced, and the **caucus system**, whereby candidates were selected in a private meeting of politicians, was replaced with the system of a more open convention. The 1828 campaign featured a great deal of rowdy advertising and much "mudslinging" on both sides. Jackson won handily, avenging his loss in 1824; he assumed office in 1829, along with his vice president, John C. Calhoun.

In his first term in office, Jackson found himself faced by a number of challenges. The first of these was initiated by the Tariff of 1828. In reaction to the tariff, John Calhoun anonymously wrote the **South Carolina Exposition and Protest**, in which he set forth in formal terms the theory of "nullification." (See the Virginia and Kentucky Resolutions of 1798.) The theory was brought to national attention in 1829 when Senator Samuel Foote suggested that the sale of lands in the west be curtailed (the **Foote Resolution**). His goal was to slow down western expansion, both to keep eastern political domination and to stop the drain of labor to the west. Obviously, those living in the west opposed this idea.

In 1830, this issue led directly to the **Webster-Hayne Debate** on the Senate floor. Senator Hayne of South Carolina, seeking an alliance with the west in which support for western land sales would be traded for support of slavery, demanded that more western land be opened for sale and suggested that nullification be employed if Congress disagreed. Senator **Daniel Webster** of Massachusetts countered with a formal repudiation of nullification for the chaos it would cause the union.

In 1832, Congress passed a new tariff that, although somewhat milder than the tariff of 1828, was still unacceptable to the South. South Carolina then did nullify it by a vote of the state legislature and threatened to secede if defied. Jackson at once announced that he was prepared to use federal troops to enforce the law. Direct confrontation was averted when Henry Clay put together a compromise whereby a new tariff (the Tariff of 1833) was voted that gradually dropped the tariff rate back down to the level it had been in 1816. Simultaneously, Congress voted for the **Force Bill**, which authorized the president to use federal troops to enforce federal law. In a face-saving move, South Carolina nullified this act, but Jackson saw fit to ignore this.

After he took office, Jackson followed a controversial practice known as the **Spoils System—** the policy of assigning government offices to one's supporters. Jackson defended this policy on the grounds that it encouraged popular participation in the election process and in government in general. He also felt that virtually all government jobs should be uncomplicated enough that they could be filled by any average citizen.

Jackson also had strong feelings concerning the rights of states to exercise sovereignty over their lands. The Indian Land Removal Act of 1830 was intended to complete the removal of Indians from lands they inhabited east of the Mississippi. However, in the case of ***Cherokee Nation v. Georgia*** (1831), the Supreme Court ruled that the Cherokees were a "domestic, dependent nation" and entitled to the land they held, within Georgia and elsewhere. Jackson refused to enforce the decision of the Court, and beginning in 1838 the Indians were driven to new reservations in the Oklahoma Territory. So many Indians perished on the trip that it became known as **The Trail of Tears**.

The institution of slavery continued to be controversial. In 1831, a black Virginia·preacher, **Nat Turner**, led an unsuccessful slave uprising in which many, both white and black, died. In reaction, Southern states tightened controls limiting the movement and education of slaves. This year also saw the beginning of the **Abolitionist Movement** with the publication of **William Lloyd Garrison**'s paper, ***The Liberator***, in Boston. Garrison called for the immediate abolition of slavery in the United States with no compensation for slaveholders. The movement gained support from others, including the sisters **Angelina and Sarah Grimke**. Daughters of a South Carolina slaveholder, they toured the northeast in the mid-1830s speaking forcefully of the oppression of slavery.

At the close of his first term, Jackson found himself faced with another challenge, this one involving the Second Bank of the United States. Jackson was opposed to the Bank in principle. He felt it to be operated in the interest of wealthy merchants along the East Coast, and it was generally assumed he would prevent it from being rechartered in 1836. However, Henry Clay decided to make the Bank's rechartering a campaign issue in 1832 by rushing through Congress a bill extending the Bank's life. Clay hoped that a Jackson veto would hurt Jackson's chances for reelection.

However, his veto did not hurt Jackson at the polls. Regardless of the financial theories involved, Jackson was largely regarded as the Common Man attacking Financial Privilege, and he won reelection easily. Considering his reelection as a mandate to eliminate the Bank at once, Jackson attacked it and its powerful president, Nicholas Biddle, by ceasing to deposit federal revenues in the Bank and withdrawing federal monies already on deposit. He then deposited these funds in various **pet banks** around the country. In turn, these banks used the funds to bankroll large loans, spurring land sales and creating a financial boom. The boom was furthered by the federal government's decision to distribute among the states the $35 million surplus that had accumulated from the tariffs and from federal land sales (money that formerly would have been deposited in the National Bank).

Late in 1836, Jackson reversed his direction. Fearful of growing trends toward speculation and debt, he issued the **Specie Circular** (specie refers to "hard money, gold and silver"), which required that all lands purchased from the national government had to be paid for with gold or silver, rather than with paper currency. This measure checked speculation, but it was also instrumental in starting a financial recession that hit the year after Jackson left office.

Also in 1836, the House of Representatives passed a measure, the **Gag Laws**, that forbade discussion of any petitions hostile to slavery. This was bitterly resented by many in the North. The prohibition remained in effect until 1844.

In the **election of 1836**, Martin Van Buren, Jackson's handpicked candidate, was elected president. He was immediately faced with the financial **Panic of 1837**, brought on in part by the Specie Circular, which quickly grew into a full-scale depression. Although this depression was not his doing, Van Buren received much of the blame. In 1840, Whig candidate William Henry Harrison, the commander at the Battle of Tippecanoe, and John Tyler (thus the campaign slogan "Tippecanoe and Tyler Too") defeated Van Buren's bid for reelection. The campaign was reminiscent of 1828 in style, and the born-in-a-log-cabin image attributed to Harrison took the place of any substantive campaign issues. This **election of 1840** was significant not only for the modern style of its public image making, but also because the Whigs, to the frustration of the Democrats, won by putting aside social elitism and openly courting "the common man." The identification of political party with social class that had marked the early Federalists receded from this point forward.

# Expansion and Social Reform (1840–1850)

William Henry Harrison caught a cold the day of his inauguration and died soon thereafter; thus John Tyler suddenly and unexpectedly became president in 1841. Though elected on the Whig ticket, Tyler was a Democrat; he had been included on the ticket to broaden its appeal to the electorate. Upon becoming president, he dismayed many by vetoing bills reestablishing a national bank and providing for internal improvements; he accepted an increased tariff in 1842 only reluctantly.

Tyler was an "expansionist," one who believed it was the **Manifest Destiny** of the United States to absorb all the lands west to the Pacific Ocean and as far north and south as it could. In northern Maine, the actual border between the United States and Canada was unclear, and loggers from both countries sought the valuable timber there. In 1840, fighting actually broke out in the area (the **Aroostook War**); however, before things got out of hand, the **Webster-Ashburton Treaty** between the U.S. and Great Britain drew a line acceptable to both sides. That line established the current boundary between Canada and the United States as far west as the Rocky Mountains.

At the same time, Texas became a focus of national attention. In the 1820s, Americans started to settle in Mexican-owned Texas at the invitation of the Mexican government. However, they began to object to the conditions of Mexico almost immediately, especially Mexico's anti-slavery position. In 1835, the Americans in Texas revolted and won their independence, becoming a separate nation in 1837 (the "Lone Star Republic"). Their application to join the United States was unsuccessful largely because many Northerners feared that such an annexation would greatly expand slave territory in the United States. In 1843, Texas again applied to join the Union. Tyler, joined by southern allies, supported the proposal; however, the treaty was defeated in the Senate by a vote of 36 to 16.

The **election of 1844** centered on the issue of expansion. The Democrat "dark horse" candidate, **James Polk**, defeated Henry Clay with a platform calling for expansionism but also pledging that slave acquisitions, such as Texas, would be balanced by free acquisitions, such as the Oregon Territory. While still in office, Tyler saw Texas annexed early in 1845.

The acquisition of Oregon proved to be more difficult because Great Britain claimed much of the territory as the result of her early fur trapping expeditions. During his campaign, Polk had pledged that the United States would gain all of the territory south of latitude 54°40' (giving rise to the cry "**54°40' or Fight!**"). This would have given the United States half of what is currently British Columbia and would have effectively cut Canada off from the Pacific Ocean. However, after winning the election and facing potential problems with Mexico to the south, Polk was in more of a mood to compromise. As a result, in 1846 both sides agreed that the 49th parallel, established by the Webster-Ashburton Treaty, would be extended to the Pacific Ocean to form the boundary between the two countries.

Meanwhile, Mexico felt that Texas still legitimately belonged to her and regarded its annexation as an act of war. Mexican officials refused even to speak with President Polk's agent, John Slidell, when he was sent to Mexico with an offer of $30 million to purchase the New Mexican Territory and California, where American settlers were seeking admission to the United States.

At this point, Polk sent **Gen. Zachary Taylor** and 2,000 troops across the Nueces River into territory still claimed by Mexico. Mexican officials demanded that the American force be withdrawn.

When it wasn't, Mexican forces entered the area, and inevitably a skirmish took place. Polk at once sent a message to Congress asking for a declaration of war and asserting that fighting had already begun "by an act of Mexico." Mexican forces were rather quickly defeated, and in 1848 Mexico signed the **Treaty of Guadalupe Hidalgo**, giving up not only her claim to Texas but also all of her land north of the Rio Grande from Texas to the Pacific Ocean for $13 million. This treaty barely managed to get the necessary two-thirds vote for ratification in the Senate. Northerners were dismayed at the possibility of still more slave states being created, while others felt that the United States should annex the whole of Mexico ("It is part of our destiny to civilize that beautiful country," editorialized the *New York Herald*).

The struggle among the sections of the United States came to the fore during the Mexican-American War. In Concord, Massachusetts, **Henry David Thoreau**, practicing what later became known as "passive resistance," went to jail (for one night) rather than pay taxes that he felt would contribute to an immoral war. In Congress, the **Wilmot Proviso**, a rider attached to a series of bills, proposed that slavery not be permitted in any lands acquired from Mexico. Opponents of the measure argued that Congress was constitutionally obligated to protect all private property, including slaves, of citizens in U.S. territories. The Proviso passed in the House of Representatives several times but was always voted down in the Senate.

Some Americans already occupied some of the land acquired from Mexico. Among these were the **Mormons**, or members of the Church of the Latter Day Saints. Joseph Smith founded this religion in western New York State in the 1820s, but some of its beliefs, particularly its espousal of polygamy, proved unpopular with its neighbors. The members were driven first to Nauvoo, Illinois, where Smith was killed, and finally, under the leadership of **Brigham Young**, to the area near the Great Salt Lake where, in 1846–1847, they established a new community. Other Americans occupying land from Mexico included federal troops that had seized the town of Santa Fe, an important trading town on the trail to California, during the war.

### Reform Movements of the 1840s

One aspect of the spirit of democracy abroad in the country during the Jacksonian years was a powerful movement toward social reform on many fronts, particularly in the north. A religious sect called the Shakers tried to establish small utopian villages in New England and New York, while Scottish industrialist **Robert Owen** also attempted to develop a utopian community based on agriculture and manufacture in New Harmony, Indiana. Strides were made in public education, with **Emma Willard** and others working to make the best level of schooling available to women. **Dorothea Dix** crusaded for improved standards in asylums for the insane, and the **American Temperance Society** began to address public problems stemming from the use of alcohol.

One of the most important of these movements was the drive for women's rights. In 1848, **Lucretia Mott** and **Elizabeth Cady Stanton** organized a conference in Seneca Falls, New York. In an eloquent *Declaration of Sentiments* patterned with pointed effect on the Declaration of Independence, they called for equal rights with men in such areas as property ownership and conditions of marriage. Some of the women there also pushed for the right to vote; others were not yet ready for that step. The **Seneca Falls Convention** was a powerful start in the movement for women's rights. Though its voice was temporarily overwhelmed in the growing furor over slavery and the approach of the Civil War, Mott and Stanton established a strong foundation for progress to be made in the second half of the century.

# Prelude to the Civil War (1850–1861)

In the **election of 1848**, neither major party wished to take a stand on the slavery issue. As a result, a splinter party, the **Free-Soil Party**, came into being with the motto of "Free Soil, Free Labor, and Free Men," and it showed some significant strength. However, the election went to Mexican War general and Southern Whig, Zachary Taylor.

In 1848, gold was discovered in California at Sutter's Mill, and all through 1849 settlers flocked to this new territory. By 1850, it was populous enough to apply for statehood. This precipitated a new crisis, since the slave-free balance in the Senate stood at 15 states apiece and there was no slave territory ready for statehood. Henry Clay, positioned between John Calhoun and the South on the one side, and the vigorous antislavery faction led by Senator William H. Seward of New York on the other, offered the following compromise (the **Compromise of 1850**):

- California was to be admitted as a free state.

- The slave trade (but not the existence of slaves) was to be forbidden within the District of Columbia.

- A strong national Fugitive Slave Law was to be passed and enforced.

- As for the other territories gained from Mexico (the New Mexican and Utah Territories), it was agreed that their status with regard to slavery would be decided by **popular sovereignty**, i.e., a vote by the residents themselves at the time the territory applied for statehood.

The compromise was bitterly debated. Finally, it received crucial support from the influential Daniel Webster, whose distaste for any extension of slavery was outweighed by his fear that the Union might come apart over this issue. His support of the compromise angered **abolitionists** in the North, but met with approval from northern businessmen and moderates. It was feared that President Taylor, who wanted both California and New Mexico to enter the Union as free states, would veto the measure, but Taylor died. **Millard Fillmore**, Taylor's vice president, became the new president and accepted the bill.

The **Fugitive Slave Act** became the chief bone of contention. Northern states consistently interfered with the law, either by passing **Personal Liberty Laws** forbidding state officials or private citizens from aiding federal courts in enforcing the act, or by aiding the **Underground Railroad**, a well-organized network of escape routes to Canada for runaway slaves. When runaway slaves were apprehended, mobs of abolitionists often made it difficult if not impossible to return them to their owners. Southerners were incensed that promises made in the Compromise of 1850 were being ignored.

Fuel was added to the fire when, in 1852, Harriet Beecher Stowe published ***Uncle Tom's Cabin***, a highly emotional novel dramatizing the plight of Southern slaves. Immensely popular in the North, it was attacked in the South as inaccurate and incendiary. However, it was a major influence preventing any easing of tension between the two sections of the country.

In the **election of 1852**, the Democrats ran Franklin Pierce, a general who had served in the Mexican War. The Whig Party found itself split along sectional lines: Southerners would accept the reelection of President Fillmore, but Northerners would not because he had accepted the hated Compromise of 1850. Finally, the Whigs settled on Winfield Scott, still another general from the Mexican-American War, but the party was badly split. After losing to Pierce and the Democrats, the Whig Party ceased to be a factor in American politics.

Pierce hoped that the Compromise of 1850 would settle the issue of slavery once and for all, but the growth of technology, specifically the railroad, prevented this from happening. For some years, the possibility of a transcontinental railroad had been discussed. In 1853, Southerners were successful in persuading the government to purchase from Mexico a strip of land along the southern border of present-day Arizona and New Mexico (the **Gadsden Purchase**), which surveyors predicted would be essential if the eastern terminus of such a railroad was to be in New Orleans.

Senator **Stephen Douglas** of Illinois was determined that the eastern terminus of the transcontinental railroad would be in Chicago. However, this would necessitate the railroad running through the Kansas and Nebraska Territories, a vast wilderness much of which lay beyond the "permanent Indian frontier," an area that, since the 1820s, had been granted to the Indians for "perpetual occupancy." In 1854, to encourage settlement of these areas, thus making it easier to convince Congress that the transcontinental railroad should begin in Illinois rather than Louisiana, Douglas ushered the **Kansas-Nebraska Act** through Congress. In order to attract Southern support, this bill specifically repealed the Missouri Compromise and provided that whether or not slavery would exist in the newly organized territories would be determined by popular sovereignty.

Supporters of slavery saw this as a golden opportunity to gain permanent control of an enormous expanse of land; abolitionists saw both a threat and a betrayal in the repeal of the Missouri Compromise. Both groups poured supporters into the Kansas Territory so as to be in the majority when the time came to vote on a constitution for statehood and thus on the issue of slavery. Soon violence broke out between the two factions. In May of 1856, the **Sack of Lawrence** occurred when pro-slavery men burned and destroyed property in the town of Lawrence, killing two people while searching for several Free-Soil leaders. A fanatical preacher named **John Brown** retaliated, attacking a pro-slavery settlement and killing five people (the **Pottawatomie Massacre**). Thereafter, a guerrilla war of sorts ensued in which more than 200 people died (**Bleeding Kansas**).

Eventually, pro-slavery forces called for a meeting in Lecompton, Kansas, to draft a constitution so that Kansas could apply for statehood. Free-Soilers boycotted the meeting, feeling that the pro-slavery forces were illegally rigging the vote. Thus the **Lecompton Constitution** permitting slavery was voted in without opposition. However, in another vote sponsored by the territorial legislature, the Free-Soil adherents rejected the constitution. Nonetheless, President James Buchanan chose to submit the Lecompton Constitution to Congress in 1858. Congress, led by Douglas, refused to go along. Kansas, therefore, remained a territory until Southern delegates walked out of Congress on the eve of the Civil War, at which point it was admitted by the remaining congressmen as a free state.

The congressional elections of 1854 were notable for the appearance of two new political parties, which between them gained a respectable number of congressional seats. One of these was the American Party, nicknamed the **Know-Nothing Party**, since its members were pledged to secrecy about party affairs. This party was formed in opposition to the rising tide of immigrants to the United States, especially those of the Roman Catholic faith. The other was the **Republican Party**, which was officially launched in July of 1854 in the Northwest and quickly swept eastward through the North in time to make a significant impression on the November elections. This party did not advocate the abolition of slavery, but it was dedicated to halting its spread to any area where it did not already exist.

Violence even broke out in the Senate of the United States. In 1856, Senator **Charles Sumner** of Massachusetts, after he had verbally insulted a Southern senator over the issue of Kansas, was physically attacked by the senator's nephew, Preston Brooks, himself a member of the House of Representatives. Sumner was beaten so severely that he was unable to return to the senate for four years. Brooks, censured by the House, was reelected unanimously by his constituency.

The presidential **election of 1856** gave another indication of the extent to which the country had become divided. James Buchanan of Pennsylvania, a Democrat, defeated John C. Fremont, running on the new Republican ticket. Buchanan won every southern state except Maryland, while Fremont's support came exclusively from the North.

In 1857, in the case of ***Dred Scott v. Sanford***, the Supreme Court attempted to settle the issue of slavery in the territories. Dred Scott, a slave, had been taken by his master to Illinois, where slavery had been illegal ever since the Northwest Ordinance of 1787, and then to the Minnesota Territory, where slavery was forbidden by the Missouri Compromise. Upon his return to Missouri, he sued for his freedom on the basis of his travels, and the case eventually reached the Supreme Court.

The actual decision of the Court was that since Scott was not a citizen of the United States, he could not legally bring suit in a federal court. If the Court had elected to stop there, the decision would have soon been forgotten. However, Chief Justice **Roger Taney**, seeking to end the controversy for good, went further. He stated that slaves were property under the terms of the Constitution, and that the federal government could not deprive a citizen of his or her property without compensation. Therefore, statutes that in any way limited slavery in territories under the authority of the national government were unconstitutional, such as the Northwest Ordinance, the Missouri Compromise, and the Kansas-Nebraska Act. The South greeted the decision with joy, the North with outrage.

This decision became the central focus in an 1858 senate race in Illinois between Stephen Douglas and Republican **Abraham Lincoln**. In a series of debates, Lincoln embarrassed Douglas by repeatedly asking him how he could reconcile the Supreme Court's decision in the Dred Scott case with his own theories of popular sovereignty. Douglas's reply, which became known as the **Freeport Doctrine**, was that although the federal government could not forbid slavery in a territory (the Dred Scott decision), the citizens therein could simply choose not to enforce the "local police regulations" necessary for slavery to survive. While Douglas won the election in a close vote, his ambiguous position cost him his southern support and any chance for the presidency; meanwhile, Lincoln's popularity in the North soared.

In 1859, another step toward disunion was taken when John Brown led an unsuccessful attempt to seize the federal arsenal at Harper's Ferry, Virginia. His plan was to use the weapons stored there to arm a slave uprising; however, federal troops under **Robert E. Lee** quickly subdued Brown and his supporters. Brown was hanged soon thereafter, but as he was eulogized in the North, the South became increasingly apprehensive of Northern threats to their **peculiar institution**.

Slavery was at the heart of the **election of 1860**. The Democratic Party split over the issue: the Northern Democrats nominated Stephen Douglas, while the Southern Democrats chose John

Breckinridge of Kentucky. The Republicans, after much infighting, chose Abraham Lincoln over William Seward and pledged not to permit any further expansion of slavery. A fourth candidate, John Bell of Tennessee, ran on the ticket of the Constitutional Union Party, a conservative group. Lincoln won only 39 percent of the total popular vote, and he failed to carry a single southern state. However, he was able to win a majority of the electoral college and therefore the presidency. On December 20, 1860, South Carolina voted to secede from the Union, and in February of 1861, seven states from the Deep South met to form the Confederate States of America.

Lame duck President Buchanan did what he could to keep things under control, including supporting the **Crittenden Amendments**, proposed amendments to the Constitution that would have guaranteed slavery where it currently existed forever and would also have reestablished the Missouri Compromise line, permitting slavery in territories south of the line. However, Lincoln refused to accept any proposal that could possibly lead to the spread of slavery, and the plan died.

# The Civil War
# (1861–1865)

Fighting between the North and the South first broke out at Fort Sumter in Charleston Harbor. While still in office, President Buchanan had sent a supply ship to the fort, but it was turned back by Confederate forces as it attempted to enter the harbor. Upon being sworn in, Lincoln redispatched the supplies, making it clear to the Confederate leaders that neither munitions nor reinforcements were included in the supplies. Thus Confederate leaders had to either permit the fort to be resupplied or fire the first shots. They chose the latter course of action, and on April 14, 1861, after two days of shelling but no casualties, the fort surrendered. In response, Lincoln called for 75,000 volunteers to put down the insurrection. Virginia and three other states of the upper South seceded at this demand and joined the states of the Confederacy.

Neither side felt that the war would last very long. The South was convinced the North would quickly tire of the effort and was also convinced that European nations, heavily dependent on Southern cotton, would intervene on the Confederate side. The South also had a low regard for the fighting ability of the average Northerner. The North, on the other hand, felt that the South's relative lack of manpower and industrial capability would soon take their toll. The North was also convinced that its naval blockade of Southern ports would succeed in cutting off Southern access to vital European supplies.

In July of 1861, the first major battle took place near Manassas, Virginia (also known as **Bull Run**), only 30 miles from Washington, DC. The inexperienced Union troops panicked and fled the field. Confederate forces, however, were not well enough organized to press their advantage. At this point, both sides began to realize that the war might not be settled as soon as they had previously thought.

Both sides recognized that the support of European nations, particularly France and Great Britain, could well be crucial for the victory. At the beginning of the war, European feelings were mixed. On the one hand, a divided United States would prove easier for Europeans to deal with; on the other hand, particularly in Great Britain, feelings against slavery ran high. A potential crisis occurred late in 1861 when a Union warship stopped a British ship, the **Trent**, on the high seas and forcibly removed two Confederate diplomats on their way to England. Great Britain vigorously protested this breech of international law; Northern leaders quickly apologized and released the Southern diplomats. (The episode became known as the **Trent Affair**.)

In 1862, Northern strategists sought to gain control of the Mississippi River, thus cutting the Confederacy in two, and by May, **David Farragut** and a Union naval squadron seized New Orleans. Union forces were also able to take Forts Henry and Donelson on the Tennessee and Cumberland Rivers, thus guaranteeing control of the upper reaches of the major river systems. **Gen. Ulysses S. Grant** then attacked Confederate forces at **Shiloh**, another town along the Tennessee River that contained crucial railroad lines, and after near defeat gained control over the area.

In the east, Union forces did not do as well. Union commander McClellan hoped to weaken Confederate resolve by marching up the peninsula and taking the Confederate capitol of Richmond (the **Peninsular Campaign**), but Confederate forces under Gen. Robert E. Lee and "Stonewall" Jackson were able to stop this advance. In September, a major confrontation took place between

Lee and McClellan at **Antietam Creek**; Lee, badly outnumbered, was able to hold on and eventually retreat with his army intact.

Conduct of the war put great pressures on Lincoln. Although he had received an active response to his original call for volunteers, that willingness dried up as the war dragged on. In 1863, Lincoln was forced to institute the first military draft in the nation's history. By the conditions of the law, a draftee could pay $300 to have someone serve in his place, so the poorer levels of Northern society began to take on a disproportionate share of the actual fighting. Against his will, Lincoln felt forced to impose on civil liberties for the sake of national security. He arrested some citizens suspected of disloyalty and jailed them without trial, in addition to censoring newspapers and private mail.

Lincoln was anxious to keep the preservation of the union rather than the abolition of slavery as the goal of the war. However, he came to see that an anti-slavery statement might be crucial in keeping European nations from intervening on behalf of the Confederacy. Just after the Battle of Antietam, he issued the **Emancipation Proclamation**, which took effect on January 1, 1863. In an attempt to persuade Confederate states to rejoin the Union, Lincoln announced that as of January 1, all slaves in areas still in rebellion against the Union would be freed; however, slaves in areas loyal to the Union, including the border states such as Missouri and Kentucky, were not affected. Accordingly, for many people the goal of the war shifted to abolishing slavery from the entire nation. It was a controversial objective, leading to bloody riots against blacks in New York City. (Slavery was finally abolished by the ratification of the **Thirteenth Amendment** in 1865.)

By June of 1863, Gen. Grant finally seized control of the town of **Vicksburg** along the Mississippi, and now Union forces controlled the entire extent of the river. Later in the year, Union forces were able to dislodge Confederate defenders at Chattanooga and thus gain control over most of eastern Tennessee along with vital railroad junctions.

In the east, Lee attempted to win a major victory, both to force Union leaders to divert men and equipment from the western campaigns and to convince European nations that the South could prove successful and therefore warranted recognition and support. At the Battle of Chancellorsville in May 1863, Lee's troops were victorious, but this was not enough. Therefore, in June, Lee took his army northward into Pennsylvania to present Union leaders with a new problem. In July, his forces met with Union troops under Gen. Meade at the small town of **Gettysburg**. For two days, the battle was indecisive, but on the third day, an all-out Confederate assault on Union positions (**Pickett's Charge**) failed, and Lee was forced to retire back into Virginia with a third of his army gone.

In 1864, Gen. Grant, now in command of all Union forces, adopted two goals. First, he ordered his western armies, under Gen. William Sherman, to march from Chattanooga to Atlanta, and from there on to Savannah on the ocean, thus subdividing the Confederacy again and demonstrating the North's overwhelming military superiority. Sherman was successful, reaching Atlanta in September and Savannah by Christmas (a campaign known as Sherman's **March to the Sea**). For his own part, Grant determined to seize Richmond, the Confederate capitol, and defeat Lee's remaining forces. Much of the spring was spent in a series of battles (Wilderness in May; Spotsylvania Court House in May; Cold Harbor in June) during which an outnumbered Lee managed to maintain a position between Grant and Richmond. The remainder of the year, both sides jockeyed for position. By the spring of 1865, with his own army down to 25,000 and with reinforcements from Sherman's army marching north to join Grant, Lee was forced to admit defeat. On April 9, he surrendered his forces to Grant at **Appomattox Court House**. The remaining Confederate forces fell soon thereafter.

Lincoln had little opportunity to savor the fruits of victory: five days after the surrender at Appomattox, he was assassinated while attending the theater. **Andrew Johnson**, a Democrat from Tennessee chosen as vice president to "balance the ticket," became president of the United States.

# The Period of Reconstruction
# (1865–1877)

With the war over, attention now focused on putting the nation back together. Abraham Lincoln had consistently argued that it was constitutionally impossible for a state to secede; therefore, it followed that the Civil War was in reality an internal rebellion by a group of individuals, not by the states themselves. By this logic, the Southern states never actually left the Union, and all that had to be done was to reestablish working governments. As early as 1863, as Union forces regained control over much of Tennessee, Louisiana, and North Carolina, Lincoln announced his **Ten Percent Plan** for restoring the South to the Union. Under this plan, most Southern citizens would be given amnesty when they took an oath of loyalty to the federal Constitution. When ten percent of the number who had voted in the election of 1860 did so, the state was permitted to rejoin the Union. Slaves were to be freed, but their future was to be left in the hands of the individual states.

The **Radical Republicans** in Congress, notably Thaddeus Stevens and Charles Sumner, disagreed with this program. They wished both to guarantee the rights of the newly freed Blacks and to punish white Southerners for the war. In 1864, they passed the **Wade-Davis Bill**, outlining their proposals. The bill called for a full majority of the citizens of a state to swear loyalty before the state could be reorganized, and it mandated that only those who could swear that they had *always* been loyal could participate in the process of writing a new state constitution. Lincoln "pocket vetoed" the measure, but the lines were drawn.

After Lincoln's assassination, Andrew Johnson supported Lincoln's proposals, and in May of 1865 he recognized new governments in Louisiana, Tennessee, Arkansas, and Virginia that had been reconstructed under the Ten Percent Plan. He also granted amnesty to many leaders of the Confederacy, thereby angering many Northerners. The newly reconstructed Southern states then passed a series of **Black Codes** designed to keep Blacks in a subservient position. Blacks were usually forbidden to bear arms, to vote, or to hold public office. In Mississippi, they could not even rent or lease land.

The Radical Republican Congress reacted swiftly, first with the **Civil Rights Act of 1866**, which attempted to define and protect the civil rights of the newly freed Blacks, and then by extending **Freedmen's Bureau**, an agency of the national government that provided emergency supplies for Blacks. Congress overrode Johnson's vetoes of both bills.

The next step taken by Congress was the introduction of the **Fourteenth Amendment**. This amendment declared that all persons born within the United States were citizens both of the national government and of the state where they lived, and it guaranteed all citizens the "due process of law." It also removed the power of the president to grant amnesty to ex-Confederate leaders, and it explicitly forbade the repayment of the Confederate debt.

In 1867, a newly elected Congress with a heavy Republican majority passed, over Johnson's vetoes, a series of bills known as the **First Reconstruction Act**. These declared illegal the governments of all the ex-Confederate states except Tennessee and organized them into five military districts, each governed by Union troops. To regain their independent status, each state had to create a new state constitution guaranteeing the civil rights of Blacks and ratifying the Fourteenth Amendment. Whites who had participated in the Civil War on the side of the Confederacy were not permitted to take part in this process.

The leaders of Congress now sought to sweep President Johnson out of office. They passed the **Tenure of Office Act**, which forbade a president from dismissing a member of his cabinet without permission from the Senate. Johnson, convinced the law was unconstitutional, dismissed his Secretary of War, Edwin Stanton, who was openly working against the president on behalf of the leaders in Congress. The House of Representatives at once voted to impeach Johnson; however, in the trial held before the Senate, the vote was one short of the two-thirds majority necessary for conviction, and Johnson remained in office.

For the most part, the South was in social, political, and economic turmoil. The plantation economy was destroyed, and the South sought to develop a new economic system overnight. Angry Southerners accused opportunistic Whites from the North (**carpetbaggers**) and from the South (**scalawags**) of taking advantage of the confusion to feather their own nests. These claims were frequently valid, although some of those accused were working sincerely to improve conditions. The emotions of the time, together with the social and economic instability of the situation, make this a very difficult matter to judge. The insecurity of Southern Whites was expressed in organizations, such as the **Ku Klux Klan**, designed to keep the Blacks "in their place."

President Grant, elected in 1868, continued the policies established in the Reconstruction Act. As a further guarantee of Blacks' rights, Congress proposed the **Fifteenth Amendment**, which guaranteed all male citizens, North and South, the right to vote; this was ratified in 1870. However, during Grant's administration, policies toward the South began to change. In 1872, Congress passed the **Amnesty Act**, restoring political rights to virtually all Southern Whites, excluding only approximately 500 top Confederate military and political officials. The result was that in many Southern states, white voters outnumbered black, and even when this wasn't the case, Whites found that economic pressure could be brought to bear to ensure white political domination. Southern Whites voted virtually unanimously for the Democratic ticket, and in 1875, Republicans found that they had lost control of the House of Representatives. Pressure to remove federal troops from the South grew; many in the North wished to forget the entire episode of the War.

In 1876, Republican **Rutherford B. Hayes** ran against New York Democrat Samuel Tilden. When the votes were finally tallied, it was found that 20 electoral votes were disputed; without these votes, Tilden was ahead by 19. The country faced a crisis, since the Constitution gave no indication of how such a situation was to be handled. Finally, a compromise was reached behind closed doors whereby all disputed votes were awarded to Hayes, making him president. In return, he agreed to withdraw the remaining troops from the South, provide some federal funds for internal improvements in the South, and guarantee a place for at least one Southerner in his cabinet. By the end of 1877, the governments of the Southern states were in the hands of Southern Whites, the **Redeemers**, as they called themselves, and Reconstruction was over.

# The Gilded Age and U.S. Imperialism (1878–1900)

## Business and Finance

Beginning in the 1850s, the United States experienced a great growth of industry. George Bissell developed an inexpensive and effective process to use oil drilled from rocks (**petroleum** = "rock oil") for lighting lamps, replacing tree sap oil, fish or whale oil, and other alternatives currently in use. The oil industry quickly sprang into being, and within a few decades **John D. Rockefeller's** Standard Oil Company had become its undisputed leader. Rockefeller attempted to gain a monopoly over all oil production in the country, and he also moved to own every aspect of the business, from the drilling rigs to the barrels in which the oil was stored to the stores in which it was sold. Other firms copied his techniques.

Also during these years, railroads spread throughout the country. The first transcontinental railroad, delayed by the Civil War, was completed in 1869, cutting down coast-to-coast travel from one month to one week. Four more transcontinental routes were completed in the next 25 years. The immense amount of money made by the railroads came not from passenger service but from shipping produce from farms and factories to the consumer, and from the substantial subsidies and bonuses granted to the railroads by the federal government. **J. P. Morgan** and **Cornelius Vanderbilt** were among the most famous and influential of the railroad tycoons.

At the same time, the steel industry was growing: a Scottish immigrant named **Andrew Carnegie** worked his way up the ladder until in 1901, he sold his Carnegie Steel Company to J. P. Morgan for more than $400 million (this in the days before income taxes). Morgan joined his new company with several smaller ones to create U.S. Steel, the country's first billion-dollar corporation. Morgan also was the dominant figure in Wall Street's banking and stock market establishment. Through a system of **interlocking directorates**, he or his close associates were connected with more than 300 of the major corporations in the country.

## The Labor Movement

The **Knights of Labor**, begun in 1869, was one of the first labor unions in the country. Its goal was to unite all workers, skilled and unskilled, black and white, together in the hopes of gaining higher wages, an eight-hour workday, and the abolition of child labor. At first, the union did not use strikes as a weapon, but by the mid-1880s, its tactics had changed. For 15 years, its influence grew under the leadership of **Terence Powderly**. However, a series of unsuccessful strikes against major railroads and public backlash against the Haymarket Massacre (see page 52) broke the union's back.

Strikes, both organized and "wildcat" (spontaneous), became common during the 1870s. In New York City, 10,000 mechanics won an eight-hour day after a strike lasting several months. In eastern Pennsylvania, certain coal miners formed a group called the **Molly McGuires** and attempted to coerce mine bosses into concessions by sending them threatening letters. In 1875, ten members of the McGuires were tried for murder, convicted on questionable evidence, and hanged. In 1877, a railroad strike began when the railroads suddenly decreased salaries by 10 percent. It quickly spread across the country. President Hayes, at the request of several governors, sent federal troops into Pennsylvania and West Virginia to end the violence.

The **American Federation of Labor** (AF of L), established in 1881 and led by **Samuel Gompers**, set the pattern for strong labor unions in the United States. Unlike the Knights of Labor, it was more a federation of skilled craft unions than an organization open to "all who toiled." Gompers made a point of distinguishing his movement from the more radical labor unions in Europe. He allowed no overtones of Marxist social revolution, emphasizing that he had no interest in overturning the capitalist system, but merely wished to gain for the workers a more equitable distribution of the profits. The AF of L preferred to use collective bargaining with management, avoiding strikes unless the union had enough financial resources to support striking workers for extended periods.

However, several significant strikes did take place. In 1886, during a strike by the Knights of Labor against the McCormick Harvester Company in Chicago, a bomb exploded at a protest meeting held in Haymarket Square, killing 7 policemen and wounding 67 others. Public opinion put the blame for the **Haymarket Massacre** on anarchists and communists. Although no concrete proof was ever found, eight anarchists were arrested and tried for the offense; four were executed. The Knights of Labor were badly scarred by this event and declined in influence.

In the 1890s, a series of strikes took place in Pennsylvania between workers and the Homestead Steel Company, a Carnegie company. Using armed guards from the Pinkerton Agency, the company attempted to break the **Homestead Strike**, and violence broke out. The Pinkertons were driven from the town; however, the Governor sent the Pennsylvania National Guard to the town to restore order, and the strike fell apart.

A similar occurrence took place at the Pullman Palace Car Company near Chicago. Here members of the American Railway Union, led by **Eugene V. Debs**, struck after their pay was cut by 25 percent. Unlike government officials in the other incidents, the Governor of Illinois, **John Atgeld**, was not sympathetic toward the owners of the company, and he did not send in state troops. However, President Cleveland was persuaded by Attorney General Olney to send in federal troops, justifying the actions on the grounds that this was necessary to guarantee delivery of federal mail. The strike was quickly broken.

### Changes Within the Social Fabric

**Urban population** grew significantly in the years following the Civil War, rising from 20 percent of the population during the Civil War to 50 percent by 1915. While the rural population rose by 200 percent, the urban population increased by 700 percent, fueled both by farmers lured to the cities by factory jobs and by immigrants from Europe. Europeans were enticed in part by lavish advertisements sponsored by the railroads that hoped the immigrants would settle the new cities and towns along their routes.

Two architectural developments enabled America's cities to absorb this population growth. **Skyscrapers** were designed to house businesses; they were made possible by the invention of elevators that could carry people above the fifth floor and by the greater availability of steel.

**Tenements** were constructed to house the poor. Originally, these were designed to house many people safely in a limited area. However, many proved unsanitary, noisy, and ill lit, producing a new variety of urban slum.

During the 1890s, historian **Frederick Jackson Turner** considered data collected by the Census Bureau in 1890, which indicated that for the first time there was an unbroken line of settlement from coast to coast, and that America's frontier had disappeared. He asserted that the frontier experience had always been crucial for the health of America's democracy. He went on to say that America's success in the past had depended on the "safety valve" of the frontier, which offered an alternative for malcontents, and that the end of the frontier would create problems for the future social adjustment of the nation. This has become known as the **Frontier Thesis**.

**Immigration and Ethnic Discrimination** became prominent issues at this time. The term *melting pot* was used during these years to describe the process by which the many different immigrant populations merged together to become "Americans." The reality was often far different: in many cases, new immigrant groups, instead of "melting" together, tended to remain in distinct ethnic clusters in the cities. One result of this was the rise of **machine politics**. By providing financial and other aid to poor immigrants, urban politicians were able to build up extremely tightly knit and loyal blocks of voters for local "bosses." When such a machine gained control of a city's government, the result was likely to be political corruption and favoritism. One famous example of this was the **Tweed Machine** in New York City, which "ruled" the city from Tammany Hall during the 1870s.

Minorities of all kinds faced discriminatory practices by "native" Americans who feared the economic competition represented by these groups. In the South, after federal troops were withdrawn in 1876, **Jim Crow Laws** were passed to enforce the segregation of Blacks in schools, public buildings, transportation, etc. These laws were challenged in the courts, but in the case of ***Plessy v. Ferguson*** (1896), the Supreme Court upheld the position of the Southern states that "separate but equal" facilities for the races were not discriminatory. In the same year, Ida Wells-Barnett formed the **National Association of Colored Women** (NACW); later she was to help found the **National Association for the Advancement of Colored People** (NAACP). Those interested in improving the lot of Blacks in America disagreed as to their tactics. Some, led by **Booker T. Washington**, were convinced that only when Blacks had proven their worth would they be accepted as equals by Whites. Therefore, he stressed programs increasing the economic status of Blacks and contributing to greater self-respect. Others formed the **Niagara Movement**, a group led by **W. E. B. DuBois**, who angrily demanded all civil rights for Blacks immediately, especially the right to vote, which although legally guaranteed by the Fifteenth Amendment, was in practice denied to Blacks widely throughout the South.

New immigrants also faced discrimination. The **Chinese Exclusion Act** was passed by Congress to limit the immigration of Chinese to the United States; many inhabitants of western states feared that they were in danger of being overwhelmed by these immigrants. The United States also moved to limit immigration from Japan when, in the **Gentlemen's Agreement** (1907), it persuaded the Japanese Government to take upon itself the prevention of such emigration. Though they complied with this agreement, the Japanese took it as a profound insult. The **Immigration Restriction League**, a group with roots in Boston's Harvard College, lobbied in Washington for a literacy test for immigrants, which would have required immigrants to be able to read and write in their own language. Such a bill passed Congress several times but was vetoed successively by Cleveland, Taft, and Wilson. It was finally passed over Wilson's veto in 1917.

**Technology and lifestyle** were also changing significantly at this time. A number of technological developments during this period substantially altered the daily life of United States citizens. Of **Thomas A. Edison's** various inventions, the electric light bulb was perhaps the most significant. It was first utilized in urban areas, moving to the farms only toward the middle of the twentieth century. For a while, the use of electricity threatened to cut into Standard Oil's profits; however, the development of the automobile in the beginning of the twentieth century produced another use for petroleum. On the farms, the government's decision to provide **Rural Free Delivery** (RFD) of mail led to mail-order shopping. Montgomery Ward and Sears Roebuck expanded the range of the rural consumer far beyond the local general store.

The landscape itself experienced some changes as rural areas gave way to company towns—sizeable towns constructed by large companies to house their workers (for example, Hershey, PA; Homestead, PA; and Pullman, IL). "Garden cities" springing up around large cities were the forerunners of modern suburbs.

A number of **reform movements** were organized during this period in addition to those pressing for minority rights. In the 1890s, **Jane Addams** established Hull House in Chicago, one of the first "settlement houses" in which people came to live among the poor in an attempt to improve the living conditions and the morale of slum life. Another reformer was **Frances Willard**, who crusaded both for the temperance movement and for women's suffrage. Although the women's movement had been launched at Seneca Falls, New York, before the Civil War, it now drew most of its support from western states, several of which gave the vote to women well before they received it nationally. Other issues involved the abolition of child labor and the improvement in the working conditions of women, especially in the "sweatshops" associated with the textile industry.

## The Frontier

Early-eighteenth-century **Indian policy** had been to force eastern tribes westward to the Great Plains, called the "Great American Desert," which was considered too desolate to be of interest to Whites. However, by the 1850s, Whites began to move into this area, too. The **Kansas-Nebraska Act** of 1854 encouraged this migration, as did the Homestead Act of 1862 (see page 55). In 1862, the Sioux tribe went on the warpath to prevent this invasion, and by 1865, in the midst of the Civil War, more than 25,000 union troops were fighting the Indians. Between 1867 and 1868, the government worked out an agreement with the Indians whereby the Indians would confine themselves to **reservations.** Although there was some resistance at first, this system seemed to work for a while. Beginning in 1871, the government stopped making official distinctions between specific tribes, and instead considered all Indians as "wards of the state."

However, in 1874, gold was discovered in the Black Hills of South Dakota; and, in violation of treaties, Whites poured into the area. The Sioux and other tribes again resorted to war. In 1876, they overwhelmed and annihilated the Seventh Calvary under **George Custer** at the Little Big Horn River. (This victory was avenged by federal troops at **Wounded Knee** in 1890 when the cavalry attacked an unarmed group of Sioux Indians, killing 200 including women and children.) In spite of Custer's defeat, the lack of cohesion among the various tribes permitted federal troops to confront and defeat small groups of Indians. Gradually, the Indians were forced back onto reservations. In 1887, Congress passed the **Dawes Act**, which sought to "Americanize" the Indian by breaking up tribal units and giving each family 160 acres of land to farm. Indians were promised that if at the end of 25 years they were successful, they would be given citizenship and free title to the land. (All Indians were finally given the rights of citizenship in 1924.)

The vast open areas of the West permitted cattle raising on a scale unheard of either in Europe or the East. After the railroad expanded to the Midwest, the "cattle drive" came into being (c. 1868–1886), whereby huge herds of cattle were driven over a thousand miles from southern Texas to railheads such as Cheyenne, Wyoming. However, the development of barbed wire allowed homesteaders to fence off the open prairies, and the spread of the railroad into Texas as well as the invention of the refrigerator car spelled the end of the cattle drive. By 1890, cattlemen began buying grazing land, fencing off the range, and practicing the business of ranching.

The signing of the **Homestead Act** of 1862 by Abraham Lincoln greatly encouraged the settlement of the West. The act gave 160 acres of land to anyone over 21 years of age provided he lived on the land and actively cultivated it. Between the years of 1870 and 1890, the population of Kansas grew from 364,000 to 1,428,000, that of Nebraska grew from 123,000 to 1,063,000, and that of the Dakota Territory grew from 2,000 to 540,000. In 1889, the last official frontier was opened for settlement in the Oklahoma Land Rush.

### Politics

The presidency of Ulysses S. Grant (1869–1877) was marred by a series of scandals. One involved the Union Pacific Railroad, which had undertaken a contract to build a transcontinental railroad from Sacramento eastward. A separate company, the **Credit Mobilier Company**, was established to handle the business, but the directors of this new company were also directors of the railroad. The new company substantially overcharged the railroad for the work done, and the excess money found its way into the pockets of the stockholders. When Congress became interested because most of the work was done with government subsidies, some congressmen who had been given stock in the Credit Mobilier at discount attempted to stall the investigation.

Questions of integrity also surrounded the **Salary Grab**, which occurred when President Grant signed a law raising both congressional and presidential salaries the evening before his second term began (the president's salary doubled), and the **Whiskey Fraud**, which involved a conspiracy between whiskey distillers and individuals in the Treasury Department to avoid paying excise tax on the liquor. In addition, the Secretary of the Navy was impeached for receiving bribes to award government contracts. These scandals served to lower the public esteem of President Grant and of the Republican Party in general.

Beginning in 1873, the country suffered a widespread depression. It was caused in part by the collapse of several companies that had invested too much in railroad development and also by heavy losses to insurance companies paying for claims as a result of two major fires in Boston and Chicago. Thousands of farmers lost their farms when they were unable to meet mortgage payments.

A persistent issue in this period was the **Currency Issue**. In 1873, the national currency, **greenbacks**, which formerly had been backed by both gold and silver, was placed completely on the gold standard. The result, since there was a limited amount of gold available, was that much of the "Gilded Age" was a period of **deflation**—over a period of time, the value of the dollar increased. While this helped some people, those with long-term debts to repay, especially farmers, were seriously hurt. (Note: A debt that would have been paid off by the proceeds of 1,000 bushels of corn in 1890 required the proceeds of 2,500 bushels in 1896.) Debtors favored one of two remedies: either issuing "greenbacks" without backing them with gold or silver, or coining unlimited amounts of silver (the so-called "free-silver" policy). In either case, the amount of currency in circulation would increase, offsetting the deflation. In 1878, Congress passed the **Bland-Allison Act**, which called for a limited coinage of silver coins with a ratio of precious metal of 16 to 1 compared to gold coins. President Hayes vetoed this as inflationary, stating that coins with less than 90 cents worth of gold per dollar were dishonest; however, Congress was able to override Hayes's veto.

Another issue dealt with **civil service**. The "Spoils System," dating back to Andrew Jackson and before, enabled victorious politicians to confer government jobs on their supporters. Hayes opposed this practice, and he attempted to have government jobs awarded on a merit basis. However, he met with substantial opposition, especially from New York Republican "Boss" Senator **Roscoe Conkling** who controlled, among others, the jobs in the New York Customhouse and gave them to party **stalwarts**. Hayes was successful in forcing the resignation of several such stalwarts, including Chester A. Arthur, but the victory was blunted when they went on to other government jobs. In the process, Hayes gained the hostility of professional politicians in his party, and he was able to accomplish little in the last two years of his administration.

In the **election of 1880**, a split developed in the Republican Party between the **Stalwarts** and the **Half-Breeds** who, while they continued to favor support for business, also favored some civil service reform and a liberal policy toward the South. The ticket agreed to was a compromise: **James Garfield**, who stood for civil service reform but avoided other issues, was nominated for president; his running partner was stalwart **Chester A. Arthur**. The Republican ticket defeated Democrat Winfield Hancock in a close election (4,454,416 to 4,444,952) despite losing every state of the "solid South." (Not until 1920 would a Republican candidate win a single Southern state.)

Garfield's administration was quite short; he was assassinated in July of 1881 by a man who sought revenge for not being given a civil service post in the administration. To the dismay of many, Chester A. Arthur became the president. (One businessman is alleged to have cried upon hearing the news that Garfield had died, "My God, Chester Arthur president!") Arthur's first annual message called for civil service reform, and Republicans in Congress responded to public sentiment after Garfield's death by supporting the **Pendleton Act**. This act set aside 14,000 government jobs (15 percent of the total) as "classified," meaning that they were to be awarded on the basis of performance on a competitive examination administered by a nonpartisan civil service administration.

When it came time to select candidates for the **election of 1884**, the Republicans passed over President Arthur and nominated James G. Blaine, a popular legislator from Maine who earlier had been accused of involvement in a railroad scandal. The Democrats selected Governor **Grover Cleveland** of New York, a political reformer. The Republicans split, one group called the **Mugwumps** defecting to the Democrats over the issues of Blaine's alleged lack of integrity. In a campaign notable for its mudslinging, Cleveland emerged victorious.

As president, Cleveland vetoed a series of bills giving Civil War pensions to those he felt did not serve them. He also began to push for lowering the tariff, which he considered an unfair form of taxation, since the government was profiting from it to the tune of $100 million a year.

Republicans opposed both of these decisions. Finally, during Cleveland's administration, the **Interstate Commerce Act** (1887) was passed, which:

- forbade railroads giving rebates or other preferential treatment to certain customers (for instance Standard Oil) to retain their business;

- required that railroad rates bear a reasonable relationship to the distance traveled;

- required that all such rates be made public and open to inspection by the Interstate Commerce Commission.

In the **election of 1888**, Representative Benjamin Harrison (grandson of President William Henry Harrison) opposed Cleveland. The central issue of the election was the tariff. Although Cleveland received more popular votes (5,540,309 to Harrison's 5,439,853), Harrison received more electoral votes and therefore won the election. Cleveland's strength was largely agricultural; Harrison scored highest in the cities.

Harrison's administration saw the passage of several major pieces of legislation. The South particularly disliked two proposed bills. The **Lodge Bill** called for the use of federal power to ensure that the right of Blacks to vote was observed, while the **McKinley Tariff Bill** called for a high protective tariff. Using the parliamentary procedure known as the **filibuster** (endless and meaningless debate prolonged on the floor to stall voting on any bill), Southern senators were able to compel the Senate to choose only one bill. The Senate ultimately passed the McKinley Tariff.

In part to soften the blow of the McKinley Tariff on the West, Congress then passed the **Sherman Silver Purchase Act**. This more than doubled the amount of silver that could be coined by the Bland-Allison Act and also called for the issue of paper money (Treasury Notes) up to the full limit of the silver coined.

Another bill that passed, the **Sherman Anti-Trust Act**, made it illegal to cause "restraint of trade or commerce" by combining businesses to form monopolies. However, the effectiveness of this law was curtailed by Supreme Court decisions that severely limited the situations in which it could be applied, and also by the reluctance of presidents before Theodore Roosevelt to apply it with vigor.

A final act passed by the Congress was the **Dependent Pension Act**, a bill that had been vetoed by Cleveland, which granted a Civil War pension to anyone who had served in the Union army for at least 90 days. Pension costs rose from $81 million to $135 million, which resulted in a depletion of the treasury surplus. This session of Congress was termed "The Billion Dollar Congress," and the country has never had an annual surplus since. The Congressional elections late in 1890 produced a landslide victory for the Democrats.

## The Populist Party

As was true in the American Revolution, farmers prospered during the Civil War and hit hard times afterward. They were hit by high railroad prices, especially prior to the Interstate Commerce Act. Farmers were forced to mortgage their farms to banks, and often lost them when they couldn't meet the payments. (Note the irony that has plagued United States farming since this time: as more cultivated land, better machinery, and new farming techniques result in increased productivity, the surplus drives prices down.)

One early association of farmers was the **Patrons of Husbandry** (1867), which formed local granges and became a sort of farmers' union, or more precisely, a number of cooperatives for buying and storing grain. These organizations supported the **Granger Laws** of the 1870s, which advocated for "cheap money" and state control over railroads through legislation. While the railroads were usually able to defeat such measures, a Supreme Court decision in 1876, *Munn v. Illinois*, declared that states had the right to regulate private property if it was "affected with a public interest," setting a precedent in the relationship between government and big business.

During the 1880s, many farmers gravitated to a variety of **Farmers' Alliances**, one of which, the Colored Farmers' Alliance, attempted to weld Black voters into an effective bloc. These groups looked to the federal government for help, rather than to the states. Distrustful of both national political parties, in 1892 they met in Omaha to form the **Populist Party**. Its platform called for:

- Free silver coinage and an increase in the money supply to $50 per person.

- A graduated income tax (see Sixteenth Amendment, page 63).

- Government regulation of all railroads and telephone and telegraph companies.

- A shorter working day for industrial workers.

- New restrictions on immigration.

- A variety of political reforms, including:
  a. The direct election of senators, who at the time were still appointed by the individual state legislatures.
  b. The initiative whereby legislation could be directly introduced by the people.
  c. The referendum, a technique whereby the voters could vote directly on specific proposals.

More generally, the Populists expressed an emotional reaction against what was perceived as "the moral, political, and material ruin of the nation."

In the **election of 1892**, three candidates ran for president. The Republicans stuck with President Harrison, the Democrats renominated former President Cleveland, and the Populists nominated James B. Weaver. Cleveland emerged victorious; however, the Populists were able to carry four states (Colorado, Nevada, Idaho, and Kansas), and they also elected 3 Senators and 11 members of the House of Representatives. Grover Cleveland became the only person to date to win two nonsuccessive presidential elections.

The beginning of Cleveland's second term saw another severe depression hit the country. The Sherman Silver Purchase Act permitted people holding treasury notes to reclaim them for gold, and many people did exactly this. Soon the government's gold supply shrunk to a dangerous level. In 1893, Cleveland called Congress into a special session to repeal the Sherman Silver Purchase Act, and after a bitter debate that split both parties, he was successful in having the act repealed.

Congress also passed a new tariff bill that was somewhat lower than the McKinley bill; Cleveland, though unenthusiastic, let it pass. The bill also included a federal income tax (2 cents for each dollar over $4,000). However, the Supreme Court, relying on the wording of Article 1, section 9 in the Constitution, declared this tax unconstitutional.

Cleveland also faced the Pullman Strike. Not only were federal troops used to protect the railroads, but in a surprising interpretation of the Sherman Anti-Trust Act, unions were defined as "a conspiracy in constraint of trade," and a court **injunction** was issued declaring workers criminals unless they stopped striking.

Following the financial **Panic of 1893**, the congressional elections of 1894 saw very strong gains for the Republicans, and also additional strength for Populist candidates.

While the repeal of the Sherman Silver Purchase Act helped slow the loss of government gold, the supply remained low. To help the situation, President Cleveland persuaded financier J. P. Morgan to arrange a massive sale of U.S. government bonds for gold, both within the United States and in Europe. The sale was successful, and the public's faith in the ability of the government to protect its currency was restored. However, many Democrats and Populists, convinced that Morgan and his fellow bankers had made an enormous profit in the transaction, were furious at Cleveland's dealings with Wall Street.

In the **election of 1896**, the Republicans, manipulated by Senator Marcus Hanna of Ohio, nominated **William McKinley**, a former congressman and current governor who was a conservative in favor of "sound money" (the gold standard), and a protective tariff. The Democrats were won over by the spectacular rhetoric of William Jennings Bryan ("You shall not press down upon the brow of labor this crown of thorns; you shall not crucify mankind upon a cross of gold!") and to the surprise of many, nominated him for president. The Populists also nominated Bryan, thus losing much of their individual identity. McKinley won the election handily; Bryan finished well in the West and the South, but failed to take a single urban-industrial state.

## William McKinley, Theodore Roosevelt, and U.S. Imperialism

Throughout much of the nineteenth century, Americans' energy and interest were focused largely on the American continent itself, especially on America's own frontier. Indeed, whether or not they approved of the nation's imperialistic ventures, beginning around 1890, most Americans recognized that these represented a radical change in the country's policies. However, in the years preceding this, there had been some involvement between the United States and less-developed territories outside its own borders.

Prompted by trade, the United States had signed formal treaties with Siam (1833) and China (1844). The Chinese treaty came in the wake of the Opium Wars in which England battered down China's resistance to trading with foreign countries. In 1852, **Admiral Perry** of the United States "opened up" Japan, using force to become the first representative of a Western power to establish trade relationships with that country in centuries. In 1854, President Pierce moved to annex both Hawaii in the Pacific and Cuba in the Caribbean, but those who feared an expansion of slavery blocked him in both cases. In 1868, under the leadership of Secretary of State William Seward, the United States purchased Alaska from Russia (the purchase became known as **Seward's Folly**). The main reason for acquiring the land at that time was the hope of squeezing England out of her possessions in western Canada.

**Pago Pago** was the occasion of America's first dispute based on imperialism of the sort Europe had been engaged in for decades. In 1889, the United States came into conflict with Germany over which power had the right to establish a **protectorate** at Pago Pago in Samoa in the South Pacific. The word *protectorate* was the formal term; the actual issue was the desirability of the spot as a fueling base for transoceanic fleets.  After a threat of war, the two nations agreed to a joint protectorate.  The incident was described by the Secretary of State in 1894 as "the first departure from our policy of avoiding entangling alliances with foreign powers in relation to objects remote from this hemisphere."

The **Organization of American States** (OAS), was formed by delegates from North, Central, and South American nations meeting in Washington in 1889 with the goal of fostering friendly relations among them.

In the 1880s, **Alfred Mahan** wrote *The Influence of Sea Power upon History*, a book that became extremely influential both within the United States and in Europe, especially England and Germany.  His thesis was that naval power, rather than armies, had determined the strength of nations throughout history, and that this was destined to continue. He made certain specific recommendations for the United States, including the building of the Panama Canal, the need to dominate the Caribbean, and the need to control both Samoa and Hawaii in the Pacific.  Two of Mahan's most enthusiastic disciples were Senator **Henry Cabot Lodge** and **Theodore Roosevelt**, a politician from New York who sought out the usually ignored position of Assistant Secretary of the Navy.

The United States became embroiled in a dispute with **Chile** when American sailors in Valparaigo were mobbed and beaten.  Chile blamed the United States for the incident and refused to pay damages.  President Harrison sent a message to Congress "seeming to invite" a declaration of war on Chile, and the United States fleet in the Pacific was readied.  Chile issued an apology and paid damages.

In **Hawaii**, the McKinley Tariff of 1890 had the effect of raising a barrier against the sale of Hawaiian sugar to the United States.  In 1893, with encouragement from President Harrison and the aid of a contingent of U.S. Marines in Honolulu, American growers in Hawaii overthrew the monarch, Queen Liluokalani, and petitioned Washington for annexation.  However, Democratic senators blocked passage of the treaty, and when President Cleveland took office in March of 1893, he called for an investigation of the incident.  After learning the extent of American involvement in the revolution, Cleveland attempted to restore the queen.  However, the American settlers were firmly in control of the Islands, and eventually Cleveland was forced to recognize the new government.  Hawaii was formally annexed to the United States in the midst of the Spanish-American War in 1898.

The **Venezuelan Border Dispute** occurred between Venezuela and Great Britain and involved disagreement over the border between Venezuela and British Guiana.  The Venezuelans sought U.S. help, and President Cleveland interpreted the **Monroe Doctrine** to say that the United States was "practically sovereign on this soil" and threatened war if the British attempted to take the disputed land by force.  However, he also urged the two countries to arbitrate the issue, which they did, largely to the eventual recognition of British claims.  Captain Mahan said of the incident, "It indicates the awakening of our countrymen to the fact that we must come out of our isolation . . . and take our share in the turmoil of the world."

In 1895, the Cuban people revolted against Spanish rule, and the Spanish reacted harshly.  The American press extensively covered the revolt, especially the widely read **Yellow Journals** owned by Joseph Pulitzer and **William Randolph Hearst**, papers more dedicated to sensationalism than objectivity.  Partly through their efforts, Americans became excited about the possibility of "freeing

Cuba"; Americans also had more than $50 million invested in Cuban sugar. Shortly after his election, President McKinley began to negotiate with Spain, and in 1897, Spain agreed to grant at least limited self-rule to the island. However, a letter from the Spanish ambassador describing McKinley as a "weak leader" was intercepted and widely publicized in the press, and then the American battleship *Maine*, anchored in Havana harbor to protect American interests, mysteriously blew up and sank. The cause of the explosion remains unknown to this day. The press accused the Spanish of having engineered the disaster and called for war, crying "Remember the *Maine*!" Theodore Roosevelt sent secret orders to the U.S. Pacific fleet to be prepared to attack the Spanish-controlled Philippines. Spain made it clear that she was prepared to agree to all reasonable American demands, but President McKinley, bowing to public opinion, accepted a Congressional declaration of war in April of 1898.

The United States quickly won the "splendid little war." With the American fleet controlling the seas, Spanish forces could not be supplied, and they had little chance against the Americans. Although American forces were disorganized and poorly equipped, they overwhelmed Spanish resistance. **Admiral Dewey's** fleet demolished the Spanish fleet at Manila in the Philippines, and Theodore Roosevelt led his **Rough Riders**, a privately organized cavalry unit, up San Juan Hill on foot, since their horses had been left in Florida by mistake. Ten times as many Americans died as a result of disease as did on the battlefield.

The war left the United States with its first colonies: Puerto Rico in the Caribbean and Guam and the Philippines in the Pacific. The Philippines posed a delicate problem because a rebel group, which had been opposing Spanish control for some time, welcomed the Americans as liberators. However, American forces put down the rebellion violently to solidify their own control over the area; the Filipinos were finally suppressed in 1902. Cuba itself was granted independence, as had been agreed to in the treaty ending the war, although Congress pressured Cuba into accepting the **Platt Amendment**, which provided that the United States could intervene directly in Cuba's affairs to preserve its independence and also gave the United States long-term leases to valuable naval bases.

America's new imperialism was a highly controversial development. To many influential citizens, imperialism represented an aggressive militarism contrary to traditional American principles, and the spectacle of the United States forcefully subdividing the Philippines was particularly distressing. In 1898, the **Anti-Imperialist League** was formed, including among its members such figures as Grover Cleveland, Harvard President Charles William Eliot, Andrew Carnegie, and Mark Twain. Nonetheless, imperialism had the decisive support of Congress and the majority of public opinion.

The United States also moved into the Far East. To get a foot in the door, Secretary of State John Hay suggested the **Open Door policy** whereby Chinese trade would be open on an equal basis to all western powers. No European nation really favored this policy, but none wished publicly to renounce it. In 1900, Chinese nationalists attempted to expel foreigners in the **Boxer Rebellion**. After they besieged the entire diplomatic corps in Peking, a joint military force including troops from the United States, Great Britain, France, Russia, Germany, and Japan invaded China and quickly put down the rebellion, winning new concessions in the process.

# Progressivism and World War I
# (1900–1920)

### Theodore Roosevelt's Administration

In the **election of 1900**, the Republicans renominated McKinley, pairing him with Rough Rider hero **Theodore Roosevelt** to lend appeal to the ticket. The Democrats again nominated William Jennings Bryan. While fiscal policy played a role, the major issue was imperialism versus **isolationism**. The Republican ticket won by a wide margin. However, five months into his second term, McKinley was assassinated by a self-proclaimed anarchist, and Theodore Roosevelt became president. (There had been a series of assassinations in the name of anarchism, both in the United States and in Europe.)

During his first term, Roosevelt found himself faced with a major coal miners' strike in West Virginia. He actively took a role in negotiating a settlement, calling both sides to the White House. He threatened the owners with federal troops unless they agreed to arbitration; they quickly backed down. In another action, Roosevelt invoked the Sherman Anti-Trust Act against the **Northern Securities Company**, a powerful railroad trust owned by J. P. Morgan, John D. Rockefeller, James J. Hill, and E. H. Harriman. The Supreme Court, by a 5–4 vote, ordered the company dissolved. Roosevelt then used the anti-trust law against other trusts in the beef, oil, and tobacco fields.

Taking an active interest in the environment, Roosevelt sponsored the **Newlands Reclamation Act**, which provided for dams and canals in the West. He also used existing presidential authority to substantially increase the amount of western land included in the nation's National Forests.

Convinced that the Spanish-American War had made clear the need for a canal through Central America, Roosevelt moved actively to initiate the **Panama Canal Project**. In 1901, the **Hay-Pauncefote Treaty** was negotiated with Great Britain, which acknowledged American right both to construct and control such a canal. Negotiations to acquire the necessary land had been held up by the high price demanded by Colombia's government, which owned Panama. When a Panamanian revolution broke out, it was quickly recognized by the United States government as the legitimate government of the region. United States troops landed in Panama to "restore order" and to prevent Colombia from resuming control. Roosevelt is reputed to have said, "I took the Canal Zone and let Congress debate it."

Roosevelt also added the **Roosevelt Corollary** to the Monroe Doctrine. Sensing a German threat to Venezuela when the latter proved unable to repay its debts, Roosevelt declared that when faced with examples of "chronic wrongdoing or impotence" in Latin American countries, the United States would intervene "however reluctantly . . . to exercise [our] international police power." When the nation of Santo Domingo was unable to repay debts to France and Italy, the United States did so intervene, controlling the nation until its debts were repaid.

In the **election of 1904**, Roosevelt easily won reelection over Democrat Alton B. Parker. The vote split along geographic lines; the North and the West went to Roosevelt, while the South voted for Parker.

During his second term, Roosevelt remained active in the world affairs. He acted as negotiator between the Japanese and the Russians to end the Russo-Japanese War, meeting with both sides at Portsmouth, New Hampshire; and at Algeciras, Spain, he helped settle a dispute between France and Germany over control of Morocco. He also sent the **Great White Fleet**, an impressive group of American warships, around the world. While presumably this was a gesture of good will, it was also a demonstration, especially to Japan, of the extent of American naval power. Soon thereafter, in the **Root-Takahira Agreement**, the United States gave Japan a free hand in Korea and Manchuria in exchange for Japan's support of the **status quo** in the Pacific.

In the domestic area, the **Hepburn Bill**, passed with difficulty over lobbying by railroads and big business, extended the authority of the Interstate Commerce Act of 1887 to pipelines, bridges, ferries and terminals, and express and sleeping car companies. It also forbade railroads from paying rebates to selected customers.

A series of books and articles by **muckrakers**, such as **Upton Sinclair's *The Jungle***, shocked the public about conditions and practices in the Chicago stockyards. The **Meat Inspection Act** and the **Pure Food and Drug Act** gave the federal government power to oversee the quality of food and drugs sold within the country.

The **Employer's Liability Act** required employers in the District of Colombia and on interstate railroads to provide accident insurance for their workers.

In 1907, a sharp business recession, the **Panic of 1907**, put pressure on President Roosevelt to ease up his attacks on large corporations. He continued to speak out for reforms, but he did not object when J. P. Morgan took steps to buy out his largest competitor.

## The Progressive Party

Much of the legislation sponsored by Theodore Roosevelt relates to a national reform movement known as the **Progressive Movement**, which can be traced back to 1889. In that year, a series of "reform mayors" were elected in several cities (Toledo, OH; Detroit, MI; and Galveston, TX), though in many cases political bosses soon reasserted control. In 1900, "Battling Bob" **Robert LaFollette** was elected Governor of Wisconsin, thus beginning a career as a political reformer that would eventually take him to the senate and to a campaign for the presidency.

The public was bombarded by the writings of the **muckrakers**, journalists and novelists who attacked corruption in business and politics as well as oppression in social conditions. Their descriptions were moving, powerful, and at times lurid. Prominent among them was Lincoln Steffens, whose *The Shame of the Cities* opened up urban areas to the scrutiny of the nation. Though he often found himself allied with them, Roosevelt felt that these journalists frequently went too far. He himself coined the term *muckraker.*

Progressive reformers met with some notable successes. In addition to the legislation mentioned above, by 1912, three quarters of the states had passed laws restricting child labor to one degree or another. In 1913, two amendments to the Constitution were ratified. The Sixteenth Amendment permitted a "graduated" income tax (the rate of which could be increased as the taxpayer's total income increased), and the Seventeenth Amendment called for United States senators to be chosen by direct popular vote rather than by state legislatures. By 1914, women's suffrage was installed in 11 states, all west of the Mississippi; and by 1917, 26 states had laws forbidding the consumption of alcohol.

Beginning in 1907, this reform movement expressed itself through the **Progressive Party**, which sometimes worked in conjunction with one of the established national parties and at other times put forth its own candidates.

Theodore Roosevelt announced well before the **election of 1908** that he would not run for reelection, and he gave his support to his handpicked successor, **William H. Taft**. Taft was easily nominated and easily won election over Democrat William Jennings Bryan, who lost a presidential race for the third time. Democrats did make some gains in Congress and among state governors, with support coming largely from farmers and industrial laborers. Following the election, former President Roosevelt left the United States for an extended big game safari in Africa and a tour of European capitals.

## William Howard Taft

During President Taft's administration, the postal service was improved, many acres of land in the Appalachian Mountains were included within the National Forests, the **Sixteenth Amendment** to the Constitution began a federal graduated income tax, and steps were taken to secure federal control over mineral resources in the United States. Forty-five indictments were filed against corporations under the anti-trust statutes. Unlike Theodore Roosevelt, Taft made no attempt to distinguish between "good" and "bad" corporations, leaving this decision up to the courts, which tended not to enforce those statutes vigorously.

In the campaign of 1908, Taft had pledged to "substantially revise" the tariff as it existed. Immediately upon taking office, he called Congress into special session to do so. The House of Representatives did pass a tariff bill with lower rates. However, the Senate, led by Senator **Aldrich** of Rhode Island, was able to attach some 800 amendments to the bill until the final version, the **Payne-Aldrich Tariff**, was very similar to the one it replaced. President Taft signed the bill without protest and even praised it in public. In so doing, he earned the censure of both the press and the Progressives among his supporters.

Taft also faced a dilemma when a disagreement broke out between **Gifford Pinchot**, Roosevelt's Chief of Forest Services, and **Richard Ballinger**, Taft's Secretary of the Interior, at this time in charge of lands with natural resources. Pinchot was a champion of Roosevelt's desire to conserve wilderness areas as a public domain and was a favorite of the former president. He accused Ballinger of favoritism when he decided to sell coal-bearing lands in Alaska to a group controlled by J. P. Morgan and Daniel Guggenheim. Convinced that Ballinger was acting in good faith, Taft stuck by him and eventually fired Pinchot.

In Congress, Progressives were determined to alter the "rules of the game" so as to gain more influence for their causes. Calling Taft "a tool of the interests," they were successful in stripping the influential and conservative Republican Speaker of the House, **Joseph Cannon**, of many of his powers, including his seat on the important House Rules Committee. They also took advantage of Taft's request for an increase in the powers of the Interstate Commerce Commission to extend its authority even farther than Taft wished.

As these controversies were being played out, Theodore Roosevelt returned to the United States fresh from a triumphant tour of Europe. Arriving amid great publicity and applause, he began to speak out in disapproval of Taft's policies. He praised the actions taken by the insurgents and called for a **New Nationalism**, which included far greater involvement of the federal government in overseeing the economy for the welfare of all the people.

In the congressional elections of 1910, the split in the Republican Party enabled the Democrats to gain control of the House of Representatives for the first time in 18 years and reduced the Republican majority in the Senate.

Taft's foreign policy strategy became known as **Dollar Diplomacy**. The government encouraged large-scale foreign investment by American corporations and then undertook to defend this investment by force. In 1912, when a civil war in Nicaragua threatened American business interests, President Taft sent in American Marines, who stilled the fighting and remained to supervise national elections. A detachment of Marines stayed in the country until late in the 1920s.

As the **election of 1912** drew near, the major attention focused on the struggle between Taft and Roosevelt for control of the Republican Party. In a hard-fought fight, Taft finally gained the nomination. In all likelihood, Roosevelt was the popular choice, but the majority of delegates to the convention were chosen by party officials loyal to the president. Roosevelt then rebelled, creating a separate party, the Progressive or **Bull-Moose Party**, with himself as the nominee. The Democrats, after some fighting of their own, nominated **Woodrow Wilson**, former president of Princeton University and reform governor of New Jersey. The campaign focused in on Roosevelt and Wilson, both seen as Progressives but with widely varying styles. Taft, a less charismatic personality, was eclipsed. While the combined total of votes for Roosevelt and Taft exceeded that for Wilson, the split between the two enabled Wilson to win an overwhelming majority of the electoral college, becoming only the second Democrat to become president since before the Civil War. (Grover Cleveland, of course, served two nonconsecutive terms.)

### Woodrow Wilson's Administration before the First World War

Domestic affairs dominated Wilson's first term in office. The **Underwood-Simmons Tariff** substantially lowered the rates of the Payne-Aldrich Tariff and tried to ensure that only industries that really needed protection received it. To make up for the revenue thus lost, an income tax bill with low rates was added to the legislation.

A major target for Wilson's progressive reforms was the nation's system for finance and banking. In 1913, the **Pujo Committee** of Congress published findings that the "money trust" involved "a web of interlocking Wall Street directorates." This report gave strong impetus to the passage of the **Federal Reserve Act**, which divided the country into 12 districts, each with its own Federal Reserve Bank owned collectively by the member banks of the district and controlled by a Federal Reserve Board appointed by the president. These Federal Reserve Banks held reserve funds of all the banks in the district, and were therefore in a position to rescue individual banks facing a "run" (a sudden, very large demand for withdrawals by depositors). The Federal Reserve also stabilized currency by issuing a new currency, **Federal Reserve Notes**, which could be printed in amounts responsive to fluctuations in the economy. This was a partial concession to the old "free-silver" proponents; William Jennings Bryan approved.

Other pieces of domestic legislation included the **Clayton Anti-Trust Act**, which went beyond the terms of the Sherman Anti-Trust Act of 1890. The new bill forbade one company from buying stock in another if it resulted in a monopoly, and also forbade one individual from holding director-ships in competing (**interlocking**) corporations. It also specifically exempted labor unions from such anti-trust prosecution. The **Federal Trade Commission Act** established the Federal Trade Commission, a five-person board to search out and prevent business practices "in restraint of trade." The **La Follette Seaman's Act** improved working conditions in the merchant marines, and the **Federal Farm Loan Act** provided farmers with long-term loans at relatively low interest rates. The **Keating-Owen Act** in 1916 prevented employment of young children in factories and mines and mandated an eight-hour workday for railroad workers. The child labor law that was in this act was quickly declared unconstitutional by the Supreme Court on the grounds that this was an area reserved to the states.

President Wilson became involved in several foreign policy episodes. In 1910, Mexican dicta-tor Porfirio Diaz was overthrown; several years later, the new leader was in turn overturned by Victoriano Huerta, a reactionary dictator. While American business interests were happy with Huerta, Wilson preferred a more democratically inclined government, referring to Huerta's coup as "immoral and illegal." After a minor incident involving several American seamen arrested in a Mexican port and at once released with apologies, Wilson sent American troops, without Congressional approval, to seize the port of Vera Cruz to redress this slight to "the rights and digni-ty" of the United States. The impending arrival of a German freighter with arms for Huerta's forces may also have been a factor in Wilson's quick decision to act. The invasion was successful, although there were losses on both sides. At this point, three Latin American countries, Argentina, Brazil, and Chile (the **ABC Powers**), arbitrated the dispute. While discussions were going on, forces under moderate Mexican leader Venustiano Carranza seized control of the country, and Huerta abdicated the presidency.

However, civil strife continued in Mexico as one of Carranza's generals, **Francisco "Pancho" Villa**, sought to overthrow the new president. Villa raided trains on both sides of the border to finance his operation. In 1916, with Carranza's reluctant permission, Wilson ordered American troops under General John Pershing to pursue Villa into Mexico. Several times this force got into clumsy skirmishes with troops loyal to Carranza. As war in Europe threatened in 1917, both Pershing and his forces were withdrawn from Mexico.

The war in Europe remained in the background during Wilson's first administration. The war broke out in August 1914, and American reaction was mixed and complex. While many instinctive-ly supported England and her allies, there was no small support for Germany, especially in parts of the Midwest, which had been settled by many people of German and Austro-Hungarian ancestry. At first, economic considerations favored the country remaining neutral so that it could trade with both sides. However, the British naval blockade on Germany coupled with Great Britain's own war needs came to influence U.S. attitudes. Between 1914 and 1916, trade with the **Allies** (Great Britain, France, and Russia, though mostly Great Britain) jumped from $800 million to more than $3 billion, while trade with Germany dropped from $170 million to approximately $1 million. Heart and pocketbook became "allied" together.

Many Americans felt that the best policy was **isolationism**. They felt that United States affairs were fundamentally separate from those of Europe and that, therefore, the United States should not become involved. American neutrality became hard-pressed, moreover, by Germany's new tactic to counter the British blockade, submarine warfare. President Wilson proclaimed that it was the right of neutrals under international law to travel wherever they wished on the high seas—even in ships of belligerent nations and into the war zone itself. The Germans claimed that if passenger ships carried war supplies, they were legitimate targets and could be attacked without warning. The sinking of the British ship *Lusitania* (a passenger ship alleged, and later proved, to be carrying war supplies) with the loss of many lives, including 128 Americans, caused a tremendous emotional response in the United States, notwithstanding the fact that the German government had purchased full-page ads in New York papers warning that they intended to attack the vessel.

Wilson protested strongly but not to the point of war. Secretary of State William Jennings Bryan was so certain that the United States was being drawn into war that he resigned; on the other hand, Theodore Roosevelt and others accused Wilson of being much too timid. After sinking the *Sussex* in the English Channel, Germany hoped to prevent American intervention in the war by agreeing to the **Sussex Pledge** to abandon their policy of attacking unarmed ships without warning.

In the **election of 1916**, Republican Charles Evans Hughes, who won the nomination over the aging Theodore Roosevelt, opposed Wilson. Wilson's platform pointed to his progressive accomplishments and to his balanced policy toward the European War: military "preparedness" coupled with the slogan, "He kept us out of war!" The final vote was very close (9,129,606 for Wilson to 8,538,221 for Hughes); the North and the East voted Republican, the South and the West voted Democratic.

## The United States and World War I

Shortly after Wilson's second administration began, several events propelled the nation toward involvement in the war. One was the decision of Germany, convinced that it could overwhelm its enemies before America's participation in the war could prove crucial, to resume "unrestricted submarine warfare" in the seas surrounding Great Britain, a practice that Wilson had already denounced. In addition, the overthrow of the Russian Tsar in the spring of 1917 and his replacement with what appeared to be a moderately democratic government made it seem possible for the United States to oppose Germany without allying itself to a repressive dictatorship. (In the fall of the same year, this moderate government was overthrown by the **Bolsheviks** under **Lenin**.) Also, the American public was greatly angered by the publication of the **Zimmermann Telegram**, a message sent by the German foreign minister to the government of Mexico. This message suggested that if the United States entered the war, Mexico's support of Germany would be rewarded by the return of her previous possessions, lost in the Mexican-American War. President Wilson asked Congress to pass the **Armed Ship Bill**, empowering the president to arm merchant ships in defense against German submarines and to take other steps to protect the nation's overseas commerce. While Congress was at first reluctant to take any steps not strictly defensive, after the publication of the Zimmermann Telegram, the House of Representatives passed the bill 403–13. In the Senate, a filibuster led by Robert LaFollette of Wisconsin prevented a vote on the bill.

Wilson found a special interpretation of an existing law that allowed him to arm the merchant ships, and he did so. However, on March 16, 1917, three American ships were sunk by the Germans, and Wilson, at a special session of Congress, declared the need to "make the world safe for democracy" and called for a declaration of war on Germany and her allies. Wilson also issued the **Fourteen Points**, a list of principles he hoped would be followed by nations after the conclusions of the war to prevent any future world confrontations. These included:

- An end to secret diplomacy and secret treaties ("open covenants, openly arrived at").

- Freedom of the seas for all nations.

- A redrawing of the national borders to permit, to the greatest degree possible, "self-determination" (the right of the peoples therein to choose their own government).

- A general disarmament of all nations.

- A League of Nations to preserve peace and handle future disagreements between nations.

### The First World War in Europe

Faced with enemies both to the east (Russia) and the west (France), Germany had attempted to defeat France early in the war in order to concentrate on the eastern front. However, after some early German victories, the fighting evolved into an extended period of **trench warfare** wherein both sides fought a series of bloody skirmishes over small bits of terrain. Through the use of submarines, Germany made a major effort to prevent Great Britain from supplying the troops on the continent.

Though the United States arrived late in the war and, in terms of casualties, suffered relatively little, the American contribution to the allied victory was significant. Almost immediately, **General John Pershing**, the American commander, made two decisions that were to have important ramifications. European allies assumed that American troops would be used as reinforcements to fill existing French and British ranks as needed; Pershing, however, insisted that U.S. troops fight as a separate and distinct unit. In addition, Pershing decided not to join in the trench warfare, emphasizing instead mobility and offensive tactics. American aid came in the nick of time, since the Bolshevik Revolution in Russia and her subsequent withdrawal from the war permitted Germany, in the fall of 1917, to concentrate all of her efforts on the "western front." However, by October of 1918, the **American Expeditionary Force** (AEF), then a million strong, had fought its way 50 miles behind the line of German trenches and controlled several railroad connections. Meanwhile, French and British troops went on the offensive, and in November, Germany signed an armistice ending the fighting.

### The Home Front

The war effort generated government regulation of daily life in ways new to the American experience. Sugar and fuel were rationed, and nonmilitary travel was discouraged. Industry was tightly regulated; the government controlled the allocation of raw materials, determined what was to be produced, and even decided upon the location of new factories. The railroad industry was **nationalized** for the duration of the war, while a **Council of Defense**, headed by **Herbert Hoover**, controlled domestic agricultural production and did much to alleviate starvation in Europe.

The war had other effects on American citizens. The **Selective Service Act** of 1917 required all men between the ages of 21 and 31 to register for the draft. Unlike the situation during the Civil War, one could not pay someone else to serve in one's place. As large numbers of men were absorbed into the military and government orders for war materials expanded, new employment opportunities developed both for women and for Blacks, many of whom moved to the north to take advantage of these jobs. Labor unions expanded, often being given government support in return for their promise not to hinder the war effort by striking.

To "mobilize minds" of Americans behind the war, the **Creel Committee** (the Committee on Public Information) was established; it published the **Official Bulletin** of the war, which contained only such information as the government chose to have publicized. Other laws were passed to "protect" America from enemy subversion. These included:

- the **Espionage Act** (1917), which gave the president wide powers of censorship and provided heavy penalties for anyone "obstructing" the war effort.

- the **Trading with the Enemy Act** (1917), which included a provision that any foreign-language newspaper published in the United States had to provide the government with an English translation.

- the **Sedition Act** (1918), which provided penalties for anyone who used "disloyal, profane, scurrilous, or abusive" language about the government, flag, or uniform; it also gave the Postmaster General the right to refuse to carry the mail of anyone who, in his opinion, was using the mail to violate this act.

## The Versailles Peace Conference

It was decided that the final peace treaty would be drawn up at a meeting held at Versailles Palace in France. President Wilson decided to attend in person, becoming the first president to leave the United States while in office. He left the United States to the cheers of crowds and arrived in Europe acclaimed a hero; he was determined to create a treaty embodying the provisions of the "Fourteen Points." It is interesting to note that his official entourage included neither Republicans nor any members of the Senate.

Wilson's idealism contrasted sharply with the pragmatism and skill of the other allied negotiators, particularly **Clemenceau** of France and **Lloyd George** of Great Britain, each of whom faced an imminent election at home. "Open covenants, openly arrived at" disappeared as Wilson was persuaded to consent to secret negotiations. "National boundaries by self-determination" was sacrificed as the victorious powers carved up minor principalities in an attempt to provide greater security for themselves. The general concept of a "peace without victory" evaporated as the allies demanded enormous **reparations**, financial payments by Germany to repay British and French war expenses. Wilson agreed to these provisions reluctantly, convinced that the establishment of the **League of Nations**, also called for in the Treaty, would eventually correct any such injustices.

When the Treaty of Versailles was published, Germans regarded it as treachery, since they had been led to believe that it would be based on Wilson's "Fourteen Points," while Americans considered it naive. Leaders such as Theodore Roosevelt and Henry Cabot Lodge argued that the Treaty could commit the nation to participate in international actions against its will, and to Wilson's great frustration and embarrassment, the Senate refused to ratify it. (Roosevelt's and Lodge's concern in this regard was quite specific. Article X of the League of Nations Charter, which would be ratified as part of the Treaty of Versailles, contained the Collective Security provision, stating that member nations would come to the aid of a member nation suffering unjust aggression.) Wilson toured the country in an unsuccessful attempt to drum up support for the Treaty and the League, and in the process he shattered his health.

Wilson declared the **election of 1920** to be a referendum on the issue of United States membership in the League of Nations, and it was accepted as such by both candidates. The Democrats nominated James M. Cox, former Governor of Ohio, and paired him with Assistant Secretary of the Navy **Franklin D. Roosevelt**; the Republicans, after a deadlock occurred between the two leading candidates, nominated "dark horse" **Warren G. Harding**. Harding, promising a "return to normalcy" and little else, won in a landslide. The United States never did ratify the Treaty of Versailles nor did it join the League of Nations. A separate peace treaty with Germany was signed in July of 1921.

# The Twenties
# (1920–1929)

**President Harding's Administration**

In 1919, before Harding was elected, a series of events took place that drew the sympathies of the American public away from foreign affairs, and away from elements perceived as foreign within American society itself.

Although the First World War had officially ended, American troops, along with contingents from England, France, and Japan, remained to fight Bolshevik forces in northern and eastern Russia in an unsuccessful attempt to topple the new regime.

During the war, unions had considered strikes unpatriotic; but now with the war over, widespread strikes broke out. In 1919, a strike of the police force in Boston was put down by Governor **Calvin Coolidge**, who then prohibited the rehiring of the strikers ("There is no right to strike against the public safety, anywhere, anytime."). The following year, Coolidge became Harding's running mate. The year 1919 also saw a series of race riots in various cities, the worst taking place in Chicago, Illinois. In addition, a series of mail bombs were sent to various political leaders, and to J. P. Morgan and John D. Rockefeller. Few did any damage.

Attorney General **A. Mitchell Palmer** blamed much of the unrest on the "prairie fire" of communism, which he alleged was sweeping the country, and he began a series of arrests and deportations of those he felt to be responsible. It is a fact that in the wake of the Russian Revolution of 1917, communist "cell groups" were established in many countries, including the United States; it is estimated that approximately 1 percent of the American adult population in 1920 were avowed communists or anarchists. Within the year, agents under Palmer's orders had arrested 6,000 people, of whom one-third were eventually released. Among those deported in the so-called **Red Scare** were 556 aliens convicted of no criminal activity. In New York, five socialists, duly elected to the state legislature, were refused the right to take their seats. A bomb was thrown at the front of the Attorney General's house, and in September of 1920, a bomb exploded at midday in front of the House of Morgan on Wall Street, killing 38 people. Soon the fear and distrust felt toward communists and other radicals spread to foreigners in general, and to native Blacks, Catholics, and Jews.

In April of 1920, a hold-up in South Braintree, Massachusetts, left two men dead. Two Italian immigrants, Nicola **Sacco** and Bartolomeo **Vanzetti**, alleged anarchists, were arrested for the crime and sentenced to death, despite inconclusive evidence. For the next six years, there were waves of protest questioning both their guilt and the severity of the punishment. In 1927, a committee formed by the governor and headed by A. Lawrence Lowell, President of Harvard and an officer of the Immigration Restriction League, concluded that while the judge had been guilty of a "grave breech of official decorum" during the trial, justice had nevertheless been done. The two men were executed.

Two constitutional amendments were ratified in 1920. The Eighteenth Amendment established **Prohibition** as the law of the land, and the Nineteenth Amendment established the right of women to exercise the **suffrage** (the right to vote). 1920 also saw the passage of an emergency immigration bill by Congress that limited the number of immigrants who could be admitted to the United States; this bill got enthusiastic support from leaders of the labor unions.

Although the United States did not join the League of Nations, it did host the **Washington Arms Conference**, held in 1921–1922 to discuss aspects of the international balance of power. The following agreements were reached:

- In the **Five Power Treaty**, the United States, Great Britain, France, Italy, and Japan agreed to control their rapidly expanding navies (especially those of Great Britain, the United States, and Japan) by limiting their "capital" ships (those over 10,000 tons) to a particular ratio. They also agreed to stop building fortresses at naval bases, except for the United States at Hawaii. The ratio permitted Great Britain and the United States 500,000 tons, Japan 300,000 tons, and France and Italy 175,000 tons. Japan in particular felt slighted by these provisions. The Treaty did nothing to control the increase in either destroyer or submarine production.

- The **Nine Power Treaty**, signed by the five major powers as well as China, Belgium, the Netherlands, and Portugal, reaffirmed the Open Door policy in China and guaranteed her sovereignty and independence.

- In the **Four Power Treaty**, the United States, Great Britain, Japan, and France agreed to respect each other's possessions in the Pacific. (The United States Senate ratified this treaty only with the stipulation that it involved no obligation to defend these possessions jointly.)

President **Harding's domestic policies** were designed to avoid a postwar recession and included lower taxes, higher tariff rates, a reduction in government spending, and aid for farmers and disabled veterans.

His tax policies received extensive Senate debate. Secretary of the Treasury Andrew Mellon advocated a repeal of wartime taxes on industry, with a decrease provided for middle- and lower-income citizens. (It was pointed out that Mellon's personal reduction would exceed that of the entire state of Nebraska.) Eventually Congress did repeal the taxes of industry, reduced taxes on the wealthy by 50 percent, and included some reductions for other income groups.

The **Fordney-McCumber Tariff** raised tariffs, discriminating against European trade to the United States at the very time European economies were struggling to recover from the war. European nations reacted by raising their own barriers to U.S. trade. The resulting stagnation in world trade contributed to the worldwide depression to come; Europeans needed trade with the United States to restore their economies so that they could repay their substantial debt to United States creditors. Great Britain and France requested that the United States cancel the $9 billion they owed as a result of war expenses. When the United States refused, these countries were forced to depend on reparation payments from Germany which, in turn, was forced to borrow from the United States to meet these payments.

President Harding's desire to limit federal spending led to the **Budget and Accounting Act**, which for the first time made the federal government accountable to budget limits established by Congress.

Veterans were given benefits of $60 and hospital expenses; however, they began to agitate for **bonus** benefits. Harding vetoed such further benefits; so did his successor, Coolidge, though the **Adjusted Compensation Act** was passed over his veto in 1924.

Beginning in 1923, President Harding found himself surrounded by a series of scandals. The president himself was not directly implicated of anything except poor judgment in the selection of his assistants, but he was shown to have little awareness of, or control over, the people immediately below him in government.

One scandal involved the Veterans Bureau, where it became clear that $250 million was missing. Bureau head Charles Forbes fled the country and resigned by cable from Europe. Meanwhile, the legal adviser to the Bureau committed suicide. Forbes was eventually brought back from Europe and jailed.

It also became obvious that the Justice Department officials were receiving bribes for various services. Jesse Smith, an aide to Attorney General Harry Daugherty, committed suicide, and Daugherty himself was tried, but not convicted, for graft. He was dismissed by Coolidge in 1924. Another member of the administration, I. W. Miller, in charge of properties confiscated from Germans in the United States during the war, was convicted of accepting bribes in return for selling these properties for less than they were worth.

**Teapot Dome** and Elk Hill were two oil reserves maintained by the federal government to stockpile naval fuel. Secretary of the Interior **Albert B. Fall** agreed to lease them to certain private oil companies; in exchange, he received $400,000 in loans and a free herd of cattle. He was convicted of bribery in 1929.

Harding himself didn't have to face all of these scandals. Just as they were beginning to surface, he left Washington for a summer trip to Alaska. He became ill en route and died in San Francisco. Vice President Calvin Coolidge thus became president. At the time of Harding's death, the whereabouts of the vice president was unknown; he was finally located fishing in Vermont and informed that he was the president.

As the **election of 1924** approached, both political parties had a rift between their rural and urban constituents. The Democrats became deadlocked at their convention, finally nominating John Davis. The Republicans saw their more progressive members split off and nominate LaFollette of Wisconsin. Still, Coolidge emerged from the confusion an easy winner. In state elections, women were elected governors in both Texas and Wyoming.

## President Coolidge's Administration

Calvin Coolidge believed in hard work, big business, and in doing nothing that wasn't clearly required, including talking. (It is said that once at a social gathering, a woman told him that she had taken a wager that she could entice him to speak more than three words; Coolidge answered, "Madam, you lose.") His policies favored big business; yet his personal honesty remained unquestioned. In accord with this sentiment, the Supreme Court issued a series of decisions favorable to business, Secretary of the Treasury Mellon continued to find taxes to cut, and Secretary of Commerce **Herbert Hoover** worked hard to help business interests, establishing along the way the **National Bureau of Standards**. In the spirit of his campaign slogan, "Keep cool with Coolidge," the president preferred to stay in the background, letting business manage itself, as it was happy to do. Little attention was paid to foreign affairs; Americans were disillusioned with the outcomes of the recent war and were convinced that the Atlantic and Pacific Oceans would serve as moats, isolating them from the world's problems.

Some of Coolidge's quotations offer a picture of the man:

"The business of America is business."

"If the federal government should go out of existence, the common run of people would not detect the difference for a considerable length of time."

"The man who builds a factory builds a temple; the man who works there worships there."

The **election of 1928** pitted Republican Herbert Hoover against Democrat **Al Smith**, the popular governor of New York. (Coolidge had withdrawn from the race with the one-line statement, "I do not choose to run.") Hoover appealed more to rural sections of the country, while Smith was more popular in the cities. Two prominent issues in the campaign were prohibition (Hoover favored it, while Smith advocated its repeal) and the fact that Smith was a Roman Catholic. The flourishing economy helped Hoover win easily; however, Smith did well in the larger cities, a foreshadowing of the urban shift to the Democratic Party.

## American Life During the 1920s

The decade following the conclusion of the war brought many significant changes to those living in the United States. The automobile became a common sight, especially as more and more roads were paved (by 1929, more than 23 million cars were in use). This permitted people to live farther from where they worked and shopped. Other inventions, such as electric refrigerators, the radio, movies (talking ones beginning in 1927), and the phonograph brought new pleasures.

Public services expanded, especially for health and education, as free elementary education became common. In the factories, **Henry Ford's** innovations, including the use of an assembly line, greatly increased production, while working conditions and safety improved.

The 1920s have been called the **Jazz Age**. This refers not only to the music that dominated the decade but to the lifestyle followed by many, particularly those living in the cities. Prohibition worked well in rural areas of the nation, but in the cities it was circumvented with ease. The "Speakeasy" became a center for social life, and the "cocktail" (a mixture of hard liquor and some sort of mixer, necessary to mask the taste of the home-brewed alcohol) replaced beer as the drink of choice, both for men and, increasingly, for women. To many older people, the younger generation was made up of dangerous radicals, with their licentious dancing and their open discussion of such topics as Freudian psychology.

Prosperity was widespread. The war years had created a tremendous reservoir of consumer demand, and factories worked overtime trying to fulfill this demand. Eventually, the increase in the goods produced considerably outran the increase in the ability of the people to pay for them. As a result, buying on credit became a common practice. During the 1920s, wages increased by 26 percent, yet consumer buying increased by 40 percent; the difference was purchased "on time." This practice was greatly stimulated by the development of sophisticated advertising as an industry in itself.

# Depression and the New Deal
# (1929–1939)

## Herbert Hoover's Administration

Hoover's presidency began on a note of optimism. The **Kellogg-Briand Pact** in 1928, signed by 66 nations, formally promised that none would use war as a means of settling international disputes; unfortunately it said nothing about what was to happen if one did. Business and industry continued to flourish. However, the production of goods continued to outstrip the increase in consumer income. People continued to purchase goods with money they did not actually possess but hoped and expected to in the future.

This tendency was particularly apparent in the area of investment. The booming growth of business had pushed the stock market up, and it encouraged people from all walks of life to buy stock on credit, by a special system called "on margin." Someone wishing to buy stock would borrow the purchase money from his or her broker. If the stock went up, the proceeds could be used to repay the debt, though usually such proceeds were reinvested to buy more stocks using the same system. If the stock went down below the original purchase price by an amount (the "margin") agreed upon in the loan contract, the broker would immediately demand payment of the original purchase price in full. Of course, in the booming **bull market** of the 1920s, neither buyer nor broker thought there was any real possibility of that happening. On paper, many such people made a great deal of money, since the increased demand for stocks pushed their prices higher and higher. However, the selling price of a stock often bore little relationship to the actual value of the company or its potential for future growth.

In September of 1929, the upward surge of the market suddenly stopped, and on October 24, the **stock market crash** occurred. Thousands of investors found that their paper profits, built up over the years, had vanished in a few hours. Late in the day, New York's most powerful bankers pooled their resources and stabilized the market by purchasing large blocks of stock at above the current selling price. However, within a few days, the market resumed its downward spiral. According to classic economic theory, when stock prices dropped to a certain point, they would become attractive bargains. People would buy them and the market would restabilize itself. The catch was that at the first wave of prices dropping below their allowed margins, brokers had demanded that investors pay up money that they could not produce. Many investors were wiped out in that first wave and had no way to buy stocks. The prices went lower and lower with no takers. In the national panic following the crash, people all over the country rushed to take their money out of banks. The banks could not handle these massive "runs" with the limited cash they kept on hand. There were widespread bank closures, and thousands of people felt that they had lost their savings altogether.

In actuality, only a distinct minority of Americans had heavily invested in stocks, and over time the nation's banks proved to be more solid than was feared in 1930. Neither the crash nor the bank runs directly caused the **Great Depression**. However, these two traumatic shocks attacked an economy that was not nearly as healthy as it had appeared. Throughout the 1920s, incomes had risen more slowly than consumer spending, so that economic growth was being driven by an increasing pattern of indebtedness. European economies had been crippled since the world war, partly because of American post-war policies. When American consumers could no longer support domestic production, there were no foreign markets to turn to, so the United States joined the depression that had been afflicting Europe for several years.

President Hoover, though philosophically convinced that government intervention in economic affairs should be strictly limited, took several steps to combat the depression. He asked congress for "a limited revision upward" of the tariff to protect domestic industry from foreign competition. In the **Hawley-Smoot Tariff**, Congress went substantially further, raising high-tariff barriers against foreign goods. The result was further stagnation of foreign trade.

On the domestic scene, the Hoover administration sought and won several pieces of legislation aimed at combating the depression.

- The **Agricultural Marketing Act** stimulated the growth of farm cooperatives and established a fund of $500 million to help stabilize farm prices by having the government purchase agricultural surpluses.

- $423 million was spent on public works, providing increased employment opportunities.

- The **Reconstruction Finance Corporation** (RFC) sought to save jobs by providing federal loans to businesses in danger of folding.

- The **Federal Home Loan Bank Act** provided federal loans to people with mortgages who were in danger of being foreclosed.

However, Hoover refused to sanction direct federal aid to individuals, feeling that it was dangerous to have people looking to the national government for charity. He said this would "injure the spiritual response of the American people." The measures Hoover took did not reverse the depression. Despite his assurances that "prosperity [was] just around the corner," many Americans were living through the darkest period of their lives.

As the depression began, the country also had to deal with new crises overseas. In 1930, at the **London Arms Conference**, the United States, Great Britain, Japan, France, and Italy met in a new attempt to hold down the rise in the world's armaments. All but Italy, then under the control of **Benito Mussolini** and his Fascist supporters, agreed to continue the terms of the Washington Conference of 1921; however, France then refused to sign the new agreement in the face of Italy's refusal. At the close of the conference, U.S. Secretary of State Stimson stated, "I am confident that with further talks we shall obtain ever-increasing security with ever-decreasing armaments."

By 1929, the Soviet Union had increased its power to the point where it began to threaten Chinese control over Northern Manchuria, and an undeclared war broke out. Attempts to end the war using the provisions of the Kellog-Briand Pact proved unsuccessful. In 1931, Japan invaded Manchuria to protect its own interests in the region and, after a brief campaign, seized control of the area. The United States expressed its opposition to this move, but took no concrete steps to counter it.

In Latin America, Hoover inherited a tradition of "dollar diplomacy." In 1912, U.S. marines had been sent into Nicaragua to protect American investments in the coffee, banana, and sugar industries. President Coolidge had withdrawn these troops in 1925, but faced with another outbreak of revolution, he sent them back almost immediately and set up a government friendly to American interests. Guerilla resistance ensued, involving the United States in a civil conflict that it proved unable to resolve. Eventually, in 1933, Hoover renounced the **Roosevelt Corollary** to the Monroe Doctrine. He promised not to intervene in Latin America's internal affairs and to recognize any government that came to power in the region. In so doing, he gained much good will in Latin America. In Mexico, a dispute over control of the nation's oil fields was averted by the diplomacy of the American ambassador. When various Latin American nations defaulted on American debts, Hoover took no retaliatory measures.

In the **election of 1932**, foreign affairs were completely overshadowed by the twin issues of depression and prohibition. The Republicans renominated Hoover; the Democrats nominated **Franklin D. Roosevelt** (FDR), a very distant cousin of Theodore Roosevelt. Roosevelt won in a landslide, carrying every state except Maine, New Hampshire, Vermont, Rhode Island, Delaware, and Pennsylvania.

## Franklin D. Roosevelt and the "New Deal"

### The First Administration

Franklin Roosevelt's overriding priority upon taking office was to rescue the economy from depression. To this end, he surrounded himself with the ablest advisers he could find, the so-called **brains trust**, both as members of his cabinet and unofficial advisers. The qualities most sought by Roosevelt were energy and a willingness to experiment, for his brain trust included widely differing points of view. (It is noteworthy that his cabinet included **Frances Perkins** as Secretary of Labor, the first woman to hold cabinet rank.)

Traditional wisdom held that in times of depression, the federal government should move to restore the confidence of the business community by balancing the budget and limiting government expenditures. During his campaign, Roosevelt had promised to balance the budget, and immediately upon taking office he proposed the **Economy Bill**, which cut government employees' salaries and veterans' pensions, and took other steps to reduce the budget deficit. He hastened the passage of the bill by supporting the Twenty-First Amendment, which, by repealing the **Volstead Act** and therefore prohibition, would serve to increase federal excise tax revenues. However, soon after the passage of the Economy Bill, Roosevelt changed his economic approach. As his **New Deal** got underway, he drew support from the theories of British economist **John Maynard Keynes**, who advocated that the government should stimulate the economy by using public expenditures to create employment, intentionally creating a deficit in the process. While Keynes's analysis provided a rationale for Roosevelt's policies, Roosevelt actually proceeded by experimentation rather than formal economic theory. Indeed, his exposure to Keynes's writings came after he was launched into his New Deal program.

**The Hundred Days** is the term applied to the first three months of Roosevelt's administration, a period during which law after law was passed by a willing Congress in the attempt to control the depression. Some of these pieces of legislation were inconsistent with others, but the overall impression of action and purpose greatly heartened the American public. During Roosevelt's first administration, a large number of bills were passed, falling into several different categories.

### • Banking and Currency

Two days after assuming office, President Roosevelt, on his own authority, ordered all American banks closed for four days to prevent any further failures. Then, with the **Emergency Banking Act**, the Secretary of the Treasury was given the authority to inspect their books and permit the sound banks to reopen with the support of the Federal Reserve System. Four-fifths of the banks quickly reopened, public "runs" for withdrawals ceased, and deposits returned, all within a few short months.

The **Glass Steagall Act** established the **Federal Deposit Insurance Corporation (FDIC)**, which insured deposits in banks affiliated with it up to $5000. It also expanded the powers of the Federal Reserve Board to limit the kind of speculation that had led to the crash.

The **Gold Reserve Act** reduced the amount of gold backing each printed dollar to 59 cents. This not only permitted the issuing of more currency, but it greatly increased the purchasing power of foreign nations, who bought with gold, thus stimulating exports while discouraging imports. (The courts upheld the constitutionality of this measure in 1935.)

The **Securities and Exchange Commission** (SEC) was established to license and regulate stock exchanges, overseeing the basic health of stocks and the practices of brokerage firms.

### • Natural Resources—Conservation

The **Civilian Conservation Corps** (CCC) offered employment to out-of-work people between the ages of 18 and 25, who worked to improve national parks and other government possessions.

The **Tennessee Valley Authority** (TVA) constructed a series of dams along the Tennessee Valley, producing a substantial amount of electrical power and providing water for irrigation. The owners of private power companies in the region vigorously opposed the project.

### • Housing

The **Home Owners' Loan Corporation** provided funds at below-market rates to refinance mortgages, while the **Federal Housing Administration** (FHA) insured mortgage loans from private banks, thus encouraging banks to make such loans.

The **Resettlement Administration** (1935) attempted to help farmers on unproductive land by resettling them on better soil; farmers were also helped by the **Farm Credit Act**, which provided federal loans specifically for farm mortgages.

### • Agriculture

The **Agricultural Adjustment Act** (AAA) sought to increase farmers' incomes by holding down the surplus. By the law of supply and demand, this action raised the price of their produce at the market. In addition, farmers who cut their acreage or who raised fewer animals would receive cash payments from the government. This money in turn came from a new tax on the industries that processed farm produce (such as mills that turned wheat to flour or cotton into cloth). These corporations were permitted to pass this additional cost onto the consumer in terms of higher prices. Thus, consumers found themselves paying twice. The goal was to achieve **parity**, a steady relationship between the price of farm produce and that of manufactured items. Between 1932 and 1935, net farm income rose by 240 percent, though this gain for one segment of society was balanced by steeper prices imposed on others.

### • Labor and Industry

A major attempt to deal with the problems of industry and labor was the establishment of the **National Recovery Administration** (NRA). Business leaders argued that existing anti-trust laws forced them into ruinous competition. The NRA suspended these laws and permitted each major industry to form an association that could set minimum prices and quotas. However, in return, the groups had to agree to regulations setting minimum wages and maximum work hours for workers. The NRA also included one section, **Section 7a**, which guaranteed organized labor the right to collective bargaining in all labor disputes. The NRA failed to satisfy everyone; small business, management, and even labor itself felt that they were uniquely disadvantaged, and all came to feel that the cumbersome restrictions accompanying the regulation were intolerable. (The NRA was quickly nicknamed the "National Run Around.") It was eventually declared unconstitutional in 1935.

Another attempt to provide work for unemployed Americans was the **Public Works Administration** (PWA) which, at considerable expense, oversaw various public works projects. Under cautious leadership, this administration proceeded very slowly; however, the **Federal Emergency Relief Act** (FERA), administered by Roosevelt's close friend **Harry Hopkins**, moved quickly to provide emergency federal relief funds for the poor, usually working through state agencies. While at times this relief was coupled with a job of some sort, at other times it took the form of direct "welfare aid." The **Civil Works Administration** (CWA) also developed public works projects; it was widely criticized for creating meaningless jobs. Within six months it was absorbed into the expending Federal Emergency Relief Act programs.

Between November 1932 and November 1934, the total government expenditures exceeded $5 billion, and the national debt doubled from its pre-depression level. On the other hand, national income rose 25 percent. Unemployment peaked at 13 million in 1933, dropped to 11 million in 1934, and to 7 million by 1936. It rose again to 11 million in 1937 as the result of a new recession (see page 81), and then dropped to below 6 million in 1941 as the nation faced the threat of a new war.

In the congressional elections of 1934, the Democrats swept Congress, winning three-quarters of the seats in the House of Representatives and two-thirds of the seats in the Senate. This margin of victory exceeded that of 1932.

Not everyone in the country agreed with the programs of Roosevelt and the Democrats, however. Former President Hoover, referring to Democratic claims that all they were proposing were the "three *R*s" (Relief, Recovery, and Reform), said that they should add a fourth: Revolution! The **American Liberty League** was made up of right-wing conservatives who opposed Roosevelt's "radicalism" and worked to protect property rights and the Constitution from the threats they perceived in New Deal policies.

The left wing also expressed its discontent. **Dr. Francis Townsend** of California gained a substantial following with his proposal to grant each American over the age of 60 a monthly pension of $200 (to be raised by a national sales tax) with the stipulation that it must be spent within the month. The so-called "Radio Priest," **Father Charles Coughlin** of Michigan, gave weekly harangues against Wall Street and the banks, calling for expansion of the country's currency and nationalization of the banking industry and natural resources. By far the most powerful figure politically was **Senator Huey Long** of Louisiana, called the "Kingfish," who won strong support in the Mississippi Valley and on the West Coast with a plan to "Share the Wealth" through heavy taxation of the wealthy. A poll taken in 1935 indicated that Long could win 3–4 million votes on a third-party ticket, thus gaining the balance of power between the two major parties; however, Long was assassinated in September 1935.

With support from the newly elected Congress, Roosevelt continued to enact legislation to deal with the depression. The **Works Progress Administration** (WPA) extended the public works program on as wide a scale as possible; it included writers, artists, and musicians in its scope. Meanwhile, the **Rural Electrification Administration** brought electric power to four-fifths of the nation's farms by 1941.

At this point, however, the New Deal faced a challenge from the Supreme Court. Although the Court had supported certain New Deal legislation, in May of 1935 it ruled that the National Recovery Administration was unconstitutional. In a case involving a poultry wholesale business in New Jersey, the Court ruled that such **intrastate** businesses could only be regulated by the individual states, and that the federal government's right to regulate **interstate** commerce did not apply. Roosevelt was furious at the "sick chicken" decision. He responded by holding Congress in special session through the summer (the **Second Hundred Days**), during which time it passed the following measures:

- Most of the NRA was allowed to go, but the **National Labor Relations Act** established an NLR board to protect and strengthen **Section 7a** of the NRA bill, guaranteeing collective bargaining and tightening restrictions on "unfair labor practices," such as attempts by management to discourage union membership.

- The **Revenue Act** (also known as the "Soak the Rich Act") raised estate and gift taxes, increased the highest possible tax on personal income to 75 percent, and made the corporate income tax proportional to the size of the company.

- The **Public Utility Holding Company Act** threatened large public utilities, such as Bell Telephone, with being dissolved unless they could prove "economies in management." This bill was challenged in the courts, but its constitutionality was upheld.

- The **Social Security Act** of 1935 provided major assistance for American workers, including:
  **a.** a federal retirement pension program with premiums being deducted from workers' salaries.
  **b.** welfare payments to the sick and elderly from general federal and state revenues.
  **c.** unemployment insurance funded by compulsory contributions from employers.

In 1936, the Supreme Court also declared the Agricultural Adjustment Act unconstitutional. Congress replied with the **Soil Conservation and Domestic Allotment Act**, which continued funneling money to farmers by paying for soil conservation measures. Concern for soil conservation was real, since severe droughts and dust storms were turning Midwest farmlands into a "dust bowl." The Court also limited the power of the Securities and Exchange Commission, struck down a bill that had made some of the NRA's coal codes into law, and declared unconstitutional a New York State law establishing a minimum wage for women. Roosevelt responded with the **Government Contracts Act**, which enabled the Secretary of Labor to set minimum wages and maximum hours for workers of firms doing business with the federal government.

By 1936, there were signs that the nation's economy was improving. Industrial production was back to the level it had reached in 1924–25, factory employment, farm income, and industrial wages were all up, and unemployment was down. The national income had raised 60 percent since 1933.

## The Second Administration

In the **election of 1936**, Roosevelt easily won a second term over Republican **Alf Landon**. The Republicans raised concern over the rise of big government, but they found it difficult to argue against many of the New Deal measures. From this point through the next 40 years, the Democrats were clearly the majority party in the nation.

In February of 1937, President Roosevelt proposed a major restructuring of the Supreme Court. Included was the suggestion that the president be authorized to name as many as six additional Justices to the Court, one for each Justice over the age of 70 who failed to resign. (The Constitution does not mandate a specific number of Justices; during the nation's history, there have been anywhere between 5 and 13.) Roosevelt's stated reason for the proposal was that the Court was behind in its work, but many were convinced his real goal was to appoint new Justices who shared his political philosophy. The proposal split the Democratic Party in Congress, as many accused Roosevelt of attempting to **pack the court**. Eventually, the Senate rejected the plan; however, conservative Justices began to retire, one during the debate and four more within the next two years. In addition, one of the more conservative Justices, Owen J. Roberts, began to vote with the liberals on close decisions, promoting the comment, "A switch in time saved nine." Thus, within a few years, Roosevelt had gained a Supreme Court willing to accept his New Deal philosophies; however, he paid a price in terms of the loss of his uncritical support from Congressional Democrats.

The **Recession of 1937** also weakened Roosevelt's support. Encouraged by signs that the economy was recovering, Roosevelt had cut 1.5 million people from the Works Projects Administration and had also encouraged the Federal Reserve Board to tighten up on credit; at the same time, the new Social Security tax lessened the amount of take-home pay enjoyed by Americans. By the end of the year, 4 million people had returned to the ranks of the unemployed. The federal government quickly returned to its free spending ways, and the recession receded, though production did not return to its mid-1937 level until during World War II.

In 1938, a **second Agricultural Adjustment Act** was enacted; it continued the benefits from the Soil Conservation Act, arranged for surplus grain to be stored by the government for use during off years, and permitted the farmers themselves to develop marketing quotas. In the same year, the **Fair Labor Standards Act** established a 40-hour workweek with "time and a half" for overtime. It established a minimum wage of 25 cents an hour; which rose to 40 cents within seven years. Seven hundred fifty thousand American workers needed raises to meet this minimum wage. The Act also prohibited those under 16 from joining the workforce. The Supreme Court did not see fit to object.

Roosevelt saw in the congressional elections of 1938 an opportunity to purge from Congress certain conservative Democrats who had joined with Republicans to block some administration proposals, in particular those extending TVA-type projects. However, his attempts backfired; Democratic conservatives and Republicans made gains. The result was that Congress became dominated by a conservative coalition; additional New Deal legislation was next to impossible.

## Social Impact of the New Deal

With the end of Reconstruction, Blacks in the South saw a steady erosion of their civil rights. Despite the words of the Fifteenth Amendment, Southern states used various techniques to discourage or prevent Blacks from voting, including:

- **Grandfather Clauses**, which stated that anyone could vote in state elections as long as they held that right on January 1, 1867 (i.e., prior to the Fifteenth Amendment) or were descended from someone who did.

- Literacy tests administered in an inconsistent way.

- Poll taxes that many poor Blacks simply found too expensive to pay.

In addition, the **Ku Klux Klan** threatened lynching and other violence for those Blacks who tried to vote, and "Jim Crow" laws kept Blacks in subservient positions.

Throughout this period, the majority of Blacks voted with the Republican Party, not because of any recent support it gave them, but because it was the traditional party of Lincoln and the Radical Reconstructionists. Blacks for the most part supported Hoover in the 1932 election and found much fault with FDR through his first term, for the social reforms of the New Deal did little to improve their situation. The various NRA codes and housing opportunities continued in practice to discriminate against Blacks, although they often included anti-discriminatory language. Roosevelt, needing the support of the Southern Democrats in Congress, didn't press the cause of Blacks. He specifically refused to force an antilynching bill on Congress, although he did speak out against the practice.

However, as Roosevelt's first term progressed, Blacks began to shift their allegiance. Even if not their strong supporter, FDR did have a number of unofficial Black advisors, while his wife, Eleanor, and his Secretary of Interior, Harold Ickes, made public gestures toward the Black community. In many cases, the direct welfare programs of the New Deal were all that poor Blacks had to survive on through the Depression. By the 1936 election, the majority of voting Blacks had shifted over to the Democratic Party, a historic realignment.

American Indians were promised their own New Deal in the **Indian Reorganization Act of 1934**. This act promised more federal aid to the reservations and a greater degree of self-government for the Indians. However, insufficient aid was actually voted, and the Bureau of Indian Affairs did little to help the situation.

On the other hand, the New Deal did make an effort to involve women in politics. There was a significant increase in the number of women holding government jobs, although few held supervisory positions. The situation was paralleled in the field of education. During the 1930s, 80 percent of public school teachers were women, but only 1.5 percent of the superintendents were women. Thirty percent of the graduate degrees went to women, but only 4 percent of the college professors were women. Women's salaries for equal jobs usually were lower than those paid to men.

Labor unions experienced a drop in membership following the 1929 crash, but began making a comeback in 1934, aided by Section 7a of the NRA. The American Federation of Labor (AF of L), founded in 1881, was the central organization, but it consisted largely of craftsmen and other skilled workers. In 1935, the **Committee for Industrial Organization** (CIO) was formed under the leadership of **John L. Lewis**; it represented steel workers, coal miners, and other relatively unskilled workers. Originally the CIO was a part of the AF of L, but it was expelled from that union in 1937 and continued aggressively on its own, organizing 4,740 strikes in 1937 alone. Unlike most unions, the CIO was open to women and to ethnic minorities. (The AF of L and the CIO merged in 1955, though friction between the two persisted.)

# World War II (1939–1945)

## The Years Before the War

The United States had entered World War I, in the words of Woodrow Wilson, "to make the world safe for democracy." However, by the middle of the 1930s, just more than a decade after the Treaty of Versailles, the outlook for democracy was bleak. Following the example of Mussolini in Italy, **Adolf Hitler** played upon the resentment felt by German people toward the Treaty of Versailles and the effect of the depression on the already weakened German economy to install a fascist government in Germany. The Soviet Union, following the death of Lenin, was under the repressive control of **Joseph Stalin**, while Japan, eager to be regarded as a world power, became increasingly under the control of its military leaders.

Despite promises by most of the major powers to avoid the use of war to solve international problems (the **Kellogg-Briand Pact** of 1928), in 1931, Japan invaded Manchuria, the northern province of China claimed by both China and the Soviet Union, setting off war with China. In 1935, Italy invaded Ethiopia in Africa, seeking imperial status. The following year civil war broke out in Spain between Fascist **General Francisco Franco**, actively supported by Germany and Italy, and Communists, actively supported by the Soviet Union and by Communist sympathizers within many European nations and the United States. Also in 1936, Hitler took over the resource-rich Rhineland, which had been a demilitarized zone since the end of World War I. European nations objected but took no concrete steps to counter the seizure.

In 1937, Japan invaded China itself, and in the process sunk the American gunboat *Panay* on the Yangtze River. In 1938, Hitler declared a union with Austria and then demanded that much of western Czechoslovakia, inhabited by several million Germans (the **Sudetenland**), be returned to German control. At a conference in Munich, Great Britain and France agreed to Hitler's demands. Soon all of the Czechoslovakia was under German control. During the spring of 1939, Hitler began to threaten Poland, which separated the main part of Germany from East Prussia and was therefore a key target for German expansion. Great Britain and France announced that they would support Polish independence, but after signing a nonaggression pact with the Soviet Union in August, Hitler invaded Poland on September 1, 1939. The Second World War had begun.

In the United States, the prevalent mood toward foreign affairs in general and events in Europe in particular was one of **isolationism**. The government adopted the **Good Neighbor Policy**, pledging not to intervene in the domestic affairs of Latin American nations. In 1933, United States troops were removed from Haiti, and the new treaty with Cuba in 1934 formally renounced the **Platt Amendment**, which had given the United States the right to intervene in Cuban affairs. Also in 1934, a timetable for the independence of the Philippines was arranged.

Congress responded to events in Europe with a series of **Neutrality Acts**. The **Nye Committee** in Congress announced that it found American intervention in World War I had been promoted to a significant degree by the fear of American businessmen and bankers that an allied defeat would threaten their profits. In 1935, impressed by these findings, Congress passed legislation that forbade America from selling arms or munitions to either side involved in war. President

Roosevelt signed the law reluctantly, expressing skepticism as to its value. The following year, Congress prohibited loans to belligerents. Further, in 1937, Congress passed a law making American civilian travel on belligerent ships illegal (to avoid another *Lusitania* incident) and limiting all trade with belligerents to a **cash-and-carry** basis (no credit and no use of American shipping). In addition, a constitutional amendment was proposed that would have forbidden a declaration of war without a public referendum; however, President Roosevelt opposed this, and the House of Representatives failed to pass it. One poll indicated that 75 percent of the American people favored this amendment.

Following Germany's seizure of Czechoslovakia, President Roosevelt asked Hitler to pledge not to attack any of 31 specified nations for the following 10 years; Hitler replied that such a pledge was unnecessary. Roosevelt then requested that Congress amend the Neutrality Acts to permit aid to Great Britain and France if they came under attack, but isolationists blocked the move. When war actually broke out in the fall of 1939, Roosevelt invoked the Neutrality Acts against both sides, but commented, "Even a neutral cannot be asked to close his mind or his conscience." He then asked, and this time received, a revision of the Neutrality Acts permitting the United States to sell arms and munitions to the allies, but only on a cash-and-carry basis. Roosevelt also provided Great Britain with badly needed destroyers by exchanging them by treaty for rights to naval bases in Canada and the West Indies.

In the **election of 1940**, despite both the fact that he broke George Washington's admonition against running for a third term and the public charm of his Republican opponent, **Wendell Wilkie**, Roosevelt won reelection easily. Wilkie attempted to focus the campaign on domestic issues, but foreign affairs dominated, with Roosevelt promising "not to send your boys to any foreign wars."

In the **Lend-Lease Act**, Roosevelt managed finally to do away with the Neutrality Laws. This new law gave the president the authority to lend or lease war supplies to a country whose defense he considered vital to the defense of the United States; thus such a country would not have to pay for such supplies with cash. By the time the act was passed in March of 1941, France had fallen to German control, Italy had joined the war on the aide of the Germans, and Great Britain found herself with her back to the wall. Shortly after the passage of Lend-Lease, Roosevelt announced to Congress his hope for "a world founded on four essential human freedoms" (the **Four Freedoms**): freedom of speech, freedom of religion, freedom from want, and freedom from fear. Later that year, after a secret meeting with Great Britain's Prime Minister, **Winston Churchill**, on a warship off the Newfoundland coast, Roosevelt issued the **Atlantic Charter**, updating Wilson's Fourteen Points.

In the meantime, friction in the Pacific was growing between the United States and Japan, largely over American demands that Japan cease its expansionist policies in China and elsewhere. In 1940, the United States placed an embargo on virtually all war materials going to Japan, including badly needed aviation fuel. Japan began negotiations with the United States to resolve their differences, but Hitler's decision to invade the Soviet Union in the spring of 1941 convinced the Japanese that their only major threat in the Pacific was the United States. On December 7, 1941, Japan launched a surprise attack on the American military base at **Pearl Harbor** in the Hawaiian Islands. The United States quickly declared war on Japan, followed shortly thereafter by similar declarations against her allies, Germany and Italy (the **Axis** powers).

## World War II

The United States entered the war none too soon for the allies. France had been defeated, and her colonies were under Axis control. England was under constant air attack (the **Battle of Britain**), and only her fighter planes and pilots offered her any protection. The United States decided almost immediately to concentrate American men and equipment in the European theater, adopting only a defensive posture against Japan in the Pacific until Germany and Italy could be subdued. From early 1942 until mid-1943, the battlefield was the Atlantic Ocean, as German submarine **wolf packs** attempted to prevent American shipping from supplying Great Britain. Gradually, the use of convoys protected by destroyers equipped with the newly invented "sonar" device began to tip the scales toward the allies; however, a tremendous tonnage was sunk with substantial loss of life.

During the summer of 1942, much attention was focused on northern Africa, where British troops attempted to halt the advance of German and Italian forces under German General **Rommel**, (known as the "Desert Fox"). Late in 1942, British forces, assisted by a joint British-American army that landed on the west coast of Africa, threw back the Axis troops and eventually contained them in Tunisia.

Meanwhile, in spite of suffering tremendous losses, Soviet troops broke a German siege at Stalingrad, capturing an entire German army in the process, and then began to push the invading German forces back westward toward Germany.

In the Pacific, following their seizure of the Philippines, Guam, Singapore, and Burma, the Japanese were mounting a threat to Australia and New Zealand. However, at the **Battle of Coral Sea** (May 1942), the Japanese advance was stopped. The battle was unique in that it was fought entirely by carrier-based planes; neither fleet ever came within sight of the other. Then, at the **Battle of Midway** in June, the Americans, having broken the Japanese code, were able to inflict heavy damage on the Japanese fleet.

In May of 1943, the German forces at Tunisia in northern Africa surrendered. This permitted an allied invasion of southern Italy, an invasion long sought by both Churchill and Stalin to divert German men and supplies from other fronts. The Italian people quickly overthrew Mussolini, and the new Italian government signed an armistice with the allied forces. However, German forces put up fierce resistance to the allied advance, and Rome wasn't conquered until May of 1944. Meanwhile, allied air forces began to conduct air attacks on Germany itself; Germany countered with "flying bombs": **V1 and V2 rockets** carrying 1-ton bombs across the channel into England.

In June of 1944, after stockpiling men and equipment in England for more than a year, allied forces under the command of U.S. General **Dwight D. Eisenhower** landed on **Normandy Beach (D-Day)** and began a steady march toward Germany, interrupted only by a short but violent German counteroffensive (the **Battle of the Bulge**) in December. By August, Paris was liberated. Meanwhile, Soviet forces invaded Germany from the east. On May 8, 1945, Germany accepted terms of "unconditional surrender." (At the Conference at Casablanca during the war it had been decided that nothing short of unconditional surrender would be accepted.)

Through 1944, United States troops in the Pacific began slowly to regain ground seized by the Japanese, "island-hopping" toward Japan itself. Many strategists had favored retaking China instead, and then using it to launch a final air assault on Japan. Much lend-lease equipment had been sent to **Generalissimo Chiang-Kai-Shek**, leader of the Chinese nationalist forces, to "keep China in the war." However, without actually opposing American proposals, Chiang managed to hoard U.S. weapons and supplies for future use against Communist insurgents.

In February of 1945, United States forces captured the island of **Iwo Jima**, and in April and May, they seized **Okinawa**. Casualties were heavy on both sides, and military experts predicted that an invasion of the Japanese mainland could cost more than a million additional American casualties. When President **Harry S Truman**, who had become president upon Roosevelt's sudden death in April of 1945, learned that the secret **Manhattan Project** had successfully developed the atomic bomb, he ordered its use first against the city of **Hiroshima** on August 6, 1945, and then, three days later, on **Nagasaki**. On August 14, 1945, the Japanese surrendered.

The Second World War saw many innovations that changed the character of war. Germany's use of mechanized land units, the "Panzer Divisions," brought new problems for those who sought to defend land masses and brought about a new description of war (the **blitzkrieg**, or "lightning war"). The use of air power completely changed the way navies confronted each other (for example, in the Battle of Coral Sea). In addition, long-range projectiles such as rockets and sophisticated bombing techniques destroyed the traditional concept of a "battlefield." Increasingly, the distinction between civilian and military became blurred. Ever since World War II, it has been a likelihood that in virtually any full-scale war, the great majority of casualties would be civilian, not military. (Korea, Vietnam, Lebanon, and El Salvador are examples.)

## The Domestic Impact of the War

The most immediate impact of the war at home was the final end to the economic recession, as industry boomed turning out war-related materials. While those at home had to put up with rationing of such items as food and gasoline and though most consumer items were in short supply, jobs abounded. **Rosie the Riveter** became a national symbol for the contribution of many women as the nation exerted its full industrial potential to build the **Arsenal of Democracy**. Jobs opened up for ethnic minorities, too, and as a result, a large number of southern Blacks migrated to northern cities. Tensions about housing and employment led to a number of urban race riots in 1943. Blacks who joined the country's military forces found themselves strictly segregated, both in terms of the units in which they served and in terms of the jobs open to them. Blacks in the navy served as waiters and kitchen help; while in the army, special platoons were established for Blacks, and they were likely to be used as mechanics and drivers. Even blood plasma of Blacks and Whites was kept separate, although no scientific reason could be found for this.

On the west coast, fear of Japanese subversion led to President Roosevelt's decision to use the army to gather up all those of Japanese ancestry, regardless of their citizenship and without any evidence whatsoever that they had committed any disloyal acts, and place them in detention centers in interior areas of the country. These people not only lost their liberty but, in many cases, most of their possessions. The Supreme Court in 1944 refused to overturn these actions.

# Truman and the Beginning of the Cold War (1945–1960)

## The Birth of the Cold War

Even while fighting was still going on during World War II, decisions were being made that would dramatically influence the postwar world.

At the **Yalta Conference**, a meeting held between Roosevelt, Churchill, and Stalin when the defeat of Germany had become inevitable, the leaders agreed that Germany would be temporarily divided into various zones administered by the Soviets, French, British, and Americans respectively. The Soviet Union was promised substantial reparations from Germany and also the vast area of Outer Mongolia, then controlled by the Japanese, as well as certain strategic Japanese island possessions. The question of the postwar governments of those Eastern European countries under German control (Poland, Czechoslovakia, Hungary, Romania, and Bulgaria) was left somewhat up in the air; the Soviets agreed to broadly based **provisional governments**, but no specifics were included as to how such governments were to be established. In exchange for these concessions, the Soviet Union agreed to enter the war against Japan within three months of the fall of Germany. Allied strategists believed that the Japanese had a large contingent of troops in Manchuria and that Soviet support would be crucial in the final defeat of Japan. The Soviet Union also agreed to participate in the soon-to-be-formed **United Nations**. President Roosevelt, recently elected to an unprecedented fourth term, was quite ill; he died within two months. Whether this affected his negotiating abilities is uncertain.

General Eisenhower made another crucial decision during the final days of the European war. Faced with the choice of pressing forward to the east so as to occupy both Berlin and Prague (thus keeping the Soviets east of these cities) or of consolidating his positions to the west of Berlin (thus avoiding additional American casualties), Eisenhower ignored Churchill's counsel and held back; Roosevelt did not question his decision. The result was that Soviet troops took possession of both Berlin and Prague, and thereby gained considerable leverage over Eastern Europe.

American possession of the **atomic bomb** seriously upset the balance of power around the world. During the war, scientists of several nations became aware of the potential of nuclear fission. As early as 1939, a group of concerned physicists alerted Albert Einstein of the possibility of a massive bomb and through him got the warning to President Roosevelt. By 1942, the **Manhattan Project** was secretly working to produce a bomb based on the chain reaction of splitting atoms. Final success didn't come until 1945, after the defeat of Germany but while Japan's substantial forces showed no signs of surrender. Truman's ultimate decision to use the weapon against the cities of Hiroshima and Nagasaki has been closely scrutinized. The twin bombings undoubtedly drew the war to a quicker close; on the other hand, it has been argued that there were alternative demonstrations that would have been equally successful without resulting in such a tremendous loss of civilian life. More than 75,000 Japanese were killed outright at Hiroshima; many more died in the coming months and years from the effects of radiation. Some have contended that in dropping the atomic bomb, Truman had the Soviet Union in mind more than Japan—he wanted to give the Soviet Union a vivid example of America's new power and to avoid having to share postwar control of Japan with the Soviet Union by subduing Japan quickly and alone. The dropping of the bomb remains a controversial issue. In any case, the United States undertook the occupation of Japan after the war, on behalf of a coalition of the victorious nations, with the Soviet Union blocked from any control there.

A final wartime conference was held at **Potsdam** in July of 1945. Truman, who only recently had become president, Churchill, and Stalin were in attendance. They agreed to try the leaders of defeated Germany as "war criminals" (the **Nuremberg Trials**); similar trials were later held in Japan. The idea of trying the leaders of a defeated nation as criminals was relatively new. The allied leaders could not agree on the future of Germany, and as a result the country was divided into a western half, controlled jointly by the United States, Great Britain, and France, and an eastern half, governed by the Soviet Union. In addition, the former capitol city of Berlin, which happened to be located within the Soviet zone, was also divided into eastern and western sections under similar controls. Other treaties drawn up at Potsdam established a democratic government in Italy but left most Eastern European countries under Soviet domination. In the Pacific, the allies agreed, as they had in Europe (in the Casablanca Conference of 1943) only to accept the "unconditional surrender" of Japan. The difficulty in reaching complete agreement amongst the victorious allies has been pointed to as an indication that the **Cold War** had begun.

## The Early Post-War Years

As the war drew to a close, the United States hosted international conferences intended to give shape to the post-war world. At **Bretton Woods** in New hampshire in the summer of 1944, forty nations agreed upon charters for the **International Monetary Fund** (IMF) and the **World Bank**. The IMF was designed to stabilize national currencies by providing a fund against which nations could borrow rather than devaluing their currencies to meet debt obligations. The World Bank could make loans for post-war reconstruction and economic growth.

Later that summer, representatives of Great Britain, the United States, France, the Soviet Union, and representatives from Chiang-Kai-Shek's government in China held a conference at **Dumbarton Oaks**, Washington, after which delegates from 50 nations met in San Francisco in 1945 and adopted a charter for the United Nations. In July of 1945, the Senate ratified the charter by a vote of 80 to 2. The new United Nations had the following components:

- A **General Assembly**, in which each nation had a single vote, regardless of size, except for the Soviet Union, which had three. Most measures were voted on by this body; however, in cases calling for the use of military force or other actions against a member state, the approval of the Security Council was required.

- The **Security Council**, comprised of five **permanent members**, the United States, the Soviet Union, China, France, and Great Britain, each with the power to veto any decision, and a number of other members (currently ten) elected for a two-year term but without the power to veto proposals.

- A **Secretariat**, headed by the **Secretary-General**, which dealt with the day-to-day affairs.

- An **International Court of Justice**, which dealt with legal issues involving member nations.

- Various agencies, usually philanthropic in nature, such as UNESCO, WHO, etc.

One immediate question facing the world was what was to become of the nuclear energy field. Congress quickly determined that research and development would remain in government hands, rather than permitting the creation of private nuclear energy companies. It established a five-man civilian board, the **Atomic Energy Commission** (AEC), to oversee its development and expansion. Within 10 years, the Commission employed 7,000 people and spent $2.5 billion annually.

In June of 1946, American Bernard Baruch sent a proposal (the **Baruch Plan**) to the newly created United Nations Atomic Energy Commission wherein the United States would turn over all of its atomic secrets to the United Nations and destroy its own stockpile of bombs if all nations agreed to outlaw the development of nuclear weapons and to permit international inspection of all atomic projects. However, the Soviet Union refused to permit such inspections within its borders and called for unilateral American destruction of its atomic capability. The Baruch plan was never put into effect.

The Soviet Union continued to plague the United States in other areas. Despite the Yalta agreements, the Soviet Union quickly installed governments in Eastern European nations sympathetic to her, creating what Winston Churchill described as an **Iron Curtain** between East and West. The Soviet Union also refused to remove troops from Iran until the United States and Great Britain threatened to use force. A Soviet spy ring was discovered in Canada, including a member of the Canadian Parliament, and rumors circulated about other instances of Russian espionage involving American atomic secrets.

President Truman also had to deal with domestic issues. Immediately after the Japanese surrender, Truman proposed to carry the New Deal forward with a program he later referred to as a **Fair Deal**. Although he encountered a more conservative Congress than Roosevelt had dealt with, he was able to pass the **Employment Act of 1946**, which confirmed in broad terms the role of government during the New Deal. It stated that it was the responsibility of the federal government "to foster and promote free competitive enterprise and the general welfare." The president became the central economic manager of the country, working with a three-person **Council of Economic Advisors**. Truman also advocated expanding social security and raising the minimum wage. Fears of massive unemployment caused by the return of the military forces to civilian life were for the most part unfounded, as industry hired new workers to meet the pent-up consumer demand, especially in the areas of automobiles and home appliances. The **G. I. Bill** of 1944 was crucial for thousands of war veterans, providing them with loans for education, homes, or the establishment of businesses.

However, inflation was a major concern. Truman asked that wartime price controls be extended in an effort to hold down consumer prices, but Congress refused. As accumulated savings flowed into the consumer market, wholesale prices for food, clothing, and fuel rose 25 percent early in 1946. This led to a series of strikes, the most serious being in the coal and railroad industries. In an attempt to force an agreement, Truman seized both industries, then asked Congress to declare a state of emergency and to legislate that strikers in a "vital industry" would lose all benefits of employment and seniority and be drafted into the army. As soldiers, these workers would be under the direct command of the president as Commander-in-Chief, and failure to obey his orders could result in a court-martial. The House of Representatives passed such legislation; however, before the Senate acted, the strikers returned to work.

In the congressional elections of 1946, the Republicans, with the slogan "Had Enough?" gained control of both houses of Congress for the first time since the depression. One prominent member of the new Congress was Senator **Robert A. Taft** of Ohio. The new Congress then passed the **Taft-**

**Hartley Act** over Truman's veto. This act dealt with labor/management issues; it allowed states to pass **Right to Work Laws** that permitted workers to refuse to join a union. It also provided for a "cooling off" period of 60 days between the time a strike was called and the time it actually began, which could be called by the president if he felt the strike would threaten the public welfare. It also forbade unions to make political contributions and required union leaders to swear they were not communists before bringing a case before the national Labor Relations Board.

Another bill enacted by Congress lowered the income tax, especially on higher incomes, again passing over Truman's veto. Congress offset the drop in federal revenues by cutting federal expenditures on farm loads, public housing, public education, and Social Security.

Truman made a variety of proposals to improve civil rights and correct racial injustice; most, however, were blocked by congressional opposition, especially among southern Democrats. On his own, he was able to desegregate the armed forces, and he appointed a black governor for the Virgin Islands and the first black federal judge.

In July of 1947, **George Kennan**, a diplomat who had served in the Soviet Union, wrote a widely read essay under the pseudonym "Mr. X," in which he suggested that a combination of the Soviet Union's paranoia over external threats from the West and the expansionist philosophy inherent in Marxist Communism made it unlikely that mere negotiation or reason would suffice to persuade her to act in accordance with American wishes. Instead, Kennan argued, the United States should be prepared to undertake a policy of **containment** whereby each attempt on the part of the Soviet Union to expand its influence would be immediately countered by the United States.

One case in point was the area surrounding the Dardanelles, the narrow passage between the Black Sea and the Mediterranean Sea controlled jointly by Greece and Turkey. The Soviet Union was putting pressure on Turkey to permit Soviet control of the area and was supplying aid to communist revolutionaries in Greece who were attempting to overthrow that government. In March of 1947, Truman called a special session of Congress and demanded $300 million for aid to Greece and $100 million for Turkey; he also called for American advisors to go to both countries to oversee the use of the money and to train troops as necessary. The new **Truman Doctrine** stated that, "It must be the policy of the United States to support free peoples who are resisting subjugation. . . . We must assist free people to work out their own destinies in their own way." The Soviet Union denounced this act as an invitation to war; however, by 1949, the threat to both countries had virtually disappeared.

Western Europe, including Great Britain, France, and Italy, also faced a threat from left-wing proponents of socialism and communism within their borders. Their economies were devastated by the war, and the resulting economic stagnation encouraged many to look to communist alternatives. In June of 1947, Secretary of State George Marshall, who had served as Army Chief of Staff during the war, announced the **Marshall Plan**, a massive influx of American aid to these countries once they had submitted a plan detailing how the aid would be spent. Congress was at first skeptical both about the expense and the principle of such international aid, but the Soviet Union's takeover of Czechoslovakia turned Congress around, and it authorized $12 billion to aid European recovery. By 1950, European productivity was 25 percent higher than it had been before the war, and the increased international trade also benefited the American economy. The Soviet Union was offered a chance to participate in the Marshall Plan but refused.

Also in 1947, the structure of the American military was reorganized. The **National Security Act** placed all military forces under a new Secretary of Defense. (The Department of Defense was created in 1949.) It also created a separate Air Force (previously part of the Army) and formed a **Joint Chiefs of Staff** as "principle military advisers" to the president. The **National Security Council** was also created to monitor national defense, relying partly on information gathered by the **Central Intelligence Agency** (CIA).

Ongoing efforts to create a unified Germany bogged down, and in June of 1948, the United States, Great Britain, and France put forth a plan to create an independent West German state. The Soviet Union reacted by establishing the **Berlin Blockade**, a prohibition of all land travel across the Soviet sector of Germany to the city of Berlin. The allied response was a continuous airlift of necessary supplies to West Berlin. After almost a year, the Soviet Union ended the blockade and proceeded to establish a comparable government in East Germany, although under close Soviet supervision.

Based on the success they had achieved in the 1946 congressional elections, Republicans felt confident of victory in the **election of 1948**. Their candidate was Governor **Thomas E. Dewey** of New York, who was liberal and charismatic. In addition, Truman's support within his own party began to break up. Even though he got the party's nomination, southern Democratic delegates, the **Dixiecrats**, broke away over the issue of Truman's civil rights record to nominate Strom Thurmond of South Carolina. Followers of Henry Wallace split off to form a new Progressive Party, protesting Truman's cold war policies toward the Soviet Union and his "loyalty checks" (see below). Polls showed Dewey so far ahead of Truman that few were taken toward the last weeks of the campaign, and one paper, the ***Chicago Tribune***, even printed the news of Dewey's victory in advance. However, partly as a result of his hard-hitting campaign oratory, Truman won a narrow popular majority and a comfortable margin in the electoral college; Democrats also regained a clear majority in the House of Representatives and a narrower one in the Senate.

## President Truman's Second Administration

America's concern with the spread of international communism overshadowed the remainder of Truman's presidency. In the midst of his first term, Truman had ordered the Federal Bureau of Investigation and the Civil Service Commission to conduct an investigation of the loyalty of all federal employees. In a four-year period that had begun in 1946, 3 million were tested and cleared, 2,900 resigned their positions, and 300 were dismissed as being of "doubtful loyalty." The Attorney General also prepared a list of 90 organizations alleged to be disloyal to the country; individuals belonging to any of these organizations were suspected of communist leanings. Largely at the insistence of Congressman **Richard M. Nixon** from California, Congress also resuscitated the **House Un-American Activities Committee** (HUAC), which had lain dormant since 1938. It began energetic investigations to root out communists in both public and private life.

One well-publicized case involved **Alger Hiss**, a former government employee who had advised Franklin Roosevelt at Yalta and who had been instrumental in setting up the United Nations at San Francisco. In 1948, a confessed Soviet spy, Whittaker Chambers, stated that he had received certain classified documents from Hiss. Hiss was accused of perjury for denying his involvement with Chambers, and though his first trial ended in a hung jury, the second in 1950 resulted in his conviction. Several ranking Democrats testified in Hiss's behalf, and Truman himself accused the House Anti-American Activities Committee and the Republican Congress of playing politics with the issue; the Republicans replied that the Democrats were "soft on communism." In September of

1949, at the height of this controversy, the Soviets exploded their first atomic weapon, several years earlier than anticipated. It was revealed that **Klaus Fuchs**, a scientist who had helped develop the bomb, had given American nuclear secrets to the Soviets between 1943 and 1947.

In his Inaugural Address in 1949, President Truman in **Point Four** called for giving economic and technical aid to nations in Asia, Africa, and Latin America along the lines of the Marshall Plan for Europe. Truman also pressed for an expanded number of projects like the Tennessee Valley Administration, a modification of the Taft-Hartly Act, and more aid for farmers and education. The Point Four Program received some funding, but those domestic programs failed to gain congressional approval.

In April of 1949, alarmed by Soviet actions in Berlin and elsewhere, 15 nations, including the United States, joined together in the **North Atlantic Treaty Association** (NATO), an alliance designed to contain any further westward expansion of Soviet influence. Congress ratified the treaty 82 to 13 after extensive debate on Article 5 of the pact, which stated that a Soviet attack on any member of the Association would be regarded as an attack on all. This was the first peacetime alliance in the history of the United States; General Dwight Eisenhower came out of retirement to become supreme military commander of NATO forces. The Soviet Union quickly countered with the **Warsaw Pact**, which tied together the military forces of the Iron Curtain countries.

For approximately 15 years prior to World War II, the political control of China had been contested by the forces of Chiang-Kai-Chek, backed economically and politically by the United States, and communist insurgents under Mao Zedong. During the war itself, both sides maintained an uneasy truce, but the close of the war brought about renewed hostilities. For several years, the United States continued to give Chiang-Kai-Chek active support; however, in 1947, after receiving a highly critical evaluation of Chiang's regime from a special envoy, Truman cut off additional aid. Toward the end of 1949, Chiang's forces were driven from the mainland to the offshore island of Formosa (Taiwan), where they were protected from further attack by an American fleet sent by Truman to keep the two adversaries apart. There was much uproar in the United States about the "loss" of China, although some observers doubted whether the United States ever had a China to lose. Most nations recognized Mao's government as ruling China, but the United States refused to do so and was able to prevent China from being represented in the United Nations.

In February of 1950, Senator **Joseph McCarthy** of Wisconsin, up for reelection in the fall, gave the first of a series of speeches in which he alleged the existence of communists in various government departments, most particularly the State Department. Working in harmony with the House Un-American Activities Committee, he quickly gathered a large following (including the young Senator from Massachusetts, **John F. Kennedy**) and an intimidating amount of political influence. It turned out that he was able to document few, if any, of his charges, but **McCarthyism** nevertheless spread well beyond Washington, leading to the **blacklisting** of many authors, performers, and educators who were unable, or unwilling, to prove their loyalty. McCarthy's "reign" continued into the Eisenhower administration. However, in 1954, when he began to accuse members of the army of having communist sympathies, the army struck back and in a series of televised congressional hearings destroyed his credibility. The result was a formal vote of censure by the Senate.

In another step to combat communism, Congress passed, over President Truman's veto, the **McCarran Internal Security Act**. This act did not make being a communist illegal, but it did:

• Require all communists and members of a "communist front" organization to register with the Attorney General.

- Force all organizations suspected of being "communist fronts" to supply the government with both membership lists and financial records.

- Forbid the employment of communists at defense plants.

- Empower the president, "in case of an internal emergency," to arrest and detain anyone suspected of being a communist.

Truman compared this act to the Sedition Act of 1798.

In the wake of the communist takeover of China, the newly formed National Security Council pressed for a more aggressive approach to the Cold War. Document **NSC-68**, approved by Truman early in 1950, called for greatly increased military spending for the rebuilding of conventional forces and the development of a hydrogen bomb. Among critics of this policy shift was George Kennan, who said his containment theory called for no such measures. However, the debate over NSC-68 was soon drowned out by events in Korea.

On June 24, 1950, North Korean troops invaded the Republic of South Korea. At the end of World War II, Korea, which had been under Japanese control, was divided between the Soviet Union in the North and the United States in the South. In 1949, the United States withdrew its troops from the south, and in January of 1950, Secretary of State Dean Acheson, discussing America's defense interests in the Pacific, gave the impression that South Korea was not an area of essential importance to the U.S. Shortly after this speech, North Korean forces launched a full-scale invasion of the South.

At the urging of the United States, the United Nation's Security Council unanimously voted to order the withdrawal of North Korean troops. (The Soviet Union was not present, since it was temporarily boycotting the UN over its refusal to seat the delegation from the new communist government in China.) Nineteen member nations of the United Nations contributed forces to the army sent to Korea to enforce the UN's orders. Eighty percent of these were American, commanded by American General **Douglas MacArthur**. President Truman never asked for congressional approval of his actions, asserting that this was not a "war" but merely a "police action" taken by the United Nations.

At first, UN forces were driven virtually into the sea; by September, they controlled only the southern tip of Korea surrounding Pusan. However, a daring landing at **Inchon** on the west coast behind communist lines was successful in breaking the North Korean advance, which after several months was forced back into North Korea. MacArthur then decided to cross over the **38th Parallel**, the line dividing North and South Korea, with the goal of reuniting the country under United Nations control, even though Communist China had warned that it would intervene if it felt threatened. On November 26, 1950, masses of Chinese troops surged over the border and threw back United Nations forces. General MacArthur argued strenuously that he should be able to expand his operations to include direct military action against China itself, including a naval blockade and aerial bombing of Chinese industrial centers. However, the Joint Chiefs of Staff, concerned about a possible Soviet counterattack in Europe, ordered MacArthur to limit his operations strictly to South Korea. MacArthur, convinced that fighting such a **limited war** played into the hands of the communists, made his feelings public in a letter to a Republican leader in the Congress; in a surprise move, on April 11, 1951, President Truman relieved MacArthur of command. MacArthur returned to the United States to receive a hero's welcome, including the opportunity to address a joint session of Congress.

At home, another case of espionage was uncovered, this time involving **Julius and Ethel Rosenberg** and **Morton Sobell**, who were accused of handing atomic secrets over to the Soviets. The Rosenbergs were sentenced to death and executed for a "crime worse than murder"; Sobell received 30 years of imprisonment. Controversy surrounded both the guilt of the accused and the severity of the sentences.

The **Anzus Pact**, based on the NATO treaty, bound the United States, Australia, and New Zealand to limit communist expansion into the South Pacific. A **Peace of Reconciliation**, developed by State Department adviser John Foster Dulles, was signed between Japan and 48 nations (not including the Soviet Union). In addition to the Peace, a separate treaty between Japan and the United States gave the U.S. the right to use military bases in Japan.

A new immigration law, the **McCarran-Walter Act**, set up quotas favoring northern and western European immigrants to the United States whereby only 2,000 Asians were permitted to immigrate annually. It also established a series of "loyalty checks" for foreigners visiting the country. The Attorney General was authorized to deport communists or members of "front" organizations even after they had become naturalized citizens. Truman vetoed the act; it passed over his veto.

In the **election of 1952**, Truman did not run for reelection; the Democrats then selected Governor **Adlai Stevenson** of Illinois. The Republicans were split between conservatives, who favored Senator Robert Taft, and the more moderate wing of the party, which managed to persuade the previously nonpolitical Dwight Eisenhower to run. Eisenhower won the nomination, and **Richard Nixon** was selected to balance the ticket. Despite Stevenson's intelligence and eloquence, he could not overcome "Ike's" wartime reputation, his obvious anti-Communist position, and his promise to end the fighting in Korea. Eisenhower won in a landslide, although the Republicans were barely able to get a majority in Congress.

## Domestic Events during the Eisenhower Administration

When Dwight D. Eisenhower became the 34th president of the United States in 1953, he also became the first president to be limited to two terms in office, the Twenty-Second Amendment to the Constitution having been ratified in 1951. His cabinet showed a definite orientation to big business. The White House staff was organized into a chain of command similar to that utilized in the military, headed by Chief of Staff **Sherman Adams**. President Eisenhower believed fervently in the free enterprise system. Wherever possible, he encouraged private enterprise and opposed governmental intrusion in the marketplace. He also favored "states rights," and he established a commission to seek out federal functions that could be returned to the states.

For many Americans, the 1950s were years of prosperity. While the nation suffered several recessions, most notably in 1953 and 1957, the real income of the American worker showed substantial improvement. Fears that the increase in automation, greatly aided by the invention of the transistor in 1947, would lead to higher unemployment turned out to be groundless, and inexpensive, abundant energy contributed to a booming economy. "The Eisenhower Era" has become an expression for this mid-1950s period of security and calm, centering largely on the style and values of middle-class suburban life. Many Americans, however, were unable to participate in such a life, while others such as **Jack Kerouac**, **Allen Ginsberg**, and other writers of the **Beat Movement** rejected the prevalent fifties values as stultifying and complacent.

The decade saw a series of significant scientific and technological advances. In 1950, the **National Science Foundation** was created to promote research. In 1953, the basic nature of genetic transmission by means of **DNA** was discovered, and by 1955, a vaccine developed by **Dr. Jonas Salk** was defeating the dreaded disease of polio. Air travel began to be widely used for long-distance travel, while the automobile began to overshadow public transit systems for commuter travel. In 1945, 31 million automobiles were registered in the nation; by 1970, the number had grown to 109 million. The Eisenhower administration gave strong support to this trend and pushed for the 1956 passage of the **Interstate Highway Act**. The result was a boom in highway construction, while relatively less was spent on systems of public transit, a trend with negative effects on major urban centers. **Television** also came into its own during this decade. In 1947, only 10,000 homes owned a television; 10 years later, the number of TV sets had grown to more than 40 million. The political potential of television was quickly recognized; Eisenhower himself was convinced to make a campaign telecast in 1952 when it was pointed out that he could reach more people in a single half hour over the airwaves than he would reach in person in several years of "whistle-stop" speeches.

While Eisenhower himself was not a leader in the movement for civil rights, one of his early appointees, Chief Justice of the Supreme Court **Earl Warren**, was. In *Brown v. The Board of Education of Topeka* in 1954, the Court unanimously overturned the "separate but equal" doctrine of *Plessy v. Ferguson* and declared that racial discrimination in education (and by inference in other institutional situations as well) was unconstitutional. Many communities, especially in the South, attempted to avoid compliance with this decision, but opponents to integration grudgingly gave in after Eisenhower sent federal troops into Little Rock, Arkansas, in 1957 to compel desegregation of the city's Central High School. Also in 1957, a **Civil Rights Act** gave federal protection to Blacks seeking to exercise the right of suffrage. (While these actions were of great historical significance, Blacks would not feel the real effectiveness of federal support for their education and voting rights until the mid-1960s.)

Southern Blacks were not dependent exclusively on the federal government for their progress in civil rights. In 1955, in Montgomery, Alabama, a 43-year-old civil rights activist named **Rosa Parks** refused to give up her seat to a white man and move to the back of the bus, as the state law required. She was arrested and fined. In protest, the black community of Montgomery began to boycott the city buses, under the leadership of the young **Reverend Martin Luther King, Jr**. Despite hardship and personal attacks, they sustained the boycott until the end of 1956, when the Supreme Court ruled that segregated busing was illegal.

By 1955, the country's economy was booming, and despite suffering a heart attack in September, by 1956, Eisenhower had recovered enough to run for a second term. In the **Election of 1956**, the Democrats again nominated Adlai Stevenson, but the result was an overwhelming victory for the Eisenhower/Nixon ticket. However, Democrats controlled the Congress.

In 1957, a recession hit the country, and in the congressional elections of 1958, the Democrats piled up a landslide. The Republicans controlled the White House, but it was obvious that this was more the result of the personal popularity of the president than popular agreement with Republican principles.

**Organized labor** became stronger in 1955 when the American Federation of Labor and the Congress for Industrial Organization merged, creating the AF of L/CIO. In 1957, a congressional investigation of the powerful maverick **Teamsters' Union** accused the union of racketeering; two years later, a **Labor Reform Act** attempted to eliminate such practices.

## Foreign Affairs 1952–1960

**John Foster Dulles** served as Secretary of State during most of Eisenhower's presidency; when he became ill in 1959, Christian Herter replaced him. Not satisfied with the idea of containment, Dulles made it clear that he intended to take the offensive against communism. Rather than depending on extensive, and expensive, conventional forces to defend America's interests around the world, Dulles introduced the concept of **massive retaliation**, the threat that if the Soviet Union took steps intolerable to the United States, the United States would respond with nuclear weapons targeted against the Soviet Union itself.

During the 1952 campaign, Eisenhower had promised "to go to Korea" if elected. He kept his promise, visiting the front before his inauguration. Early in 1953, Stalin died, and hopes ran high that the new Soviet leader, **Georgi Malenkof**, would be less antagonistic. On July 27, 1953, an armistice was signed at **Punmunjom** between North Korea and United Nations forces; both sides withdrew behind a line running roughly along the 38th Parallel. Talks were scheduled to devise a plan to reunify the country; however, they were never held, and the armistice became an uneasy truce that continues today.

By 1954, the allies had become convinced that the reunification of Germany was impossible, and France was finally persuaded to permit West Germany to regain its sovereignty and to begin at least limited rearmament.

In 1955, the leaders of the United States, Great Britain, France, and the Soviet Union convened a **summit meeting** at Geneva, Switzerland, and the rhetoric appeared much less bellicose, encouraging many to hope that a permanent thaw in the cold war had occurred. However, few substantive agreements were reached. In 1956, these hopes were dashed when the Soviet Union violently put down the **Hungarian Revolution**. The United States protested Soviet actions in Hungary and praised the "Hungarian patriots," but America gave no physical assistance to the rebels.

In October of 1957, the Soviet Union stunned the Western world by launching *Sputnik*, a small satellite, which proved beyond doubt that the Soviets had made substantial progress in the field of rocketry. The United States had taken comfort in the fact that while the Soviet Union had nuclear weapons, it didn't appear to have a delivery system that could threaten the United States itself. However, **international ballistic missiles** changed this. Worry about a possible **missile gap** led to a substantial increase in the resources devoted to missile research and to scientific study in general, and it was also a major issue in the election of 1960. One step taken in 1958 was the establishment of the **National Aeronautics and Space Administration** (NASA).

1959 saw another slight thaw in U.S./Soviet relations when **Nikita Khrushchev**, who had emerged as the Soviet Union's ruler, paid a cordial visit to the United States (although he was unable to visit Disneyland, as he had requested, because of security problems). Another **summit meeting** was planned in Paris in May of 1960; however, Khrushchev angrily disbanded the meeting in protest over an American U-2 spy plane that had been making "overflights" of the Soviet Union and was shot down. President Eisenhower lost some credibility because he at first denied the incident and only acknowledged American responsibility for the plane when the evidence became irrefutable.

The debate between the **Asia Firsters**, who felt that America's primary emphasis should be in developing her position in Asia, and those who felt that European affairs should receive priority continued through the Eisenhower years. Indochina served to focus these arguments. At the end of World War II, control over this region (which included the countries of Laos, Cambodia, and Vietnam) had switched from Japan to France, the region's former colonial overlord. Almost at once, an indigenous liberation movement broke out under the leadership of communist **Ho Chi Minh**. By 1954, French forces, even with substantial material aid from the United States, found themselves surrounded at a fortress named **Dien Bien Phu**, and they requested immediate American military assistance. Eisenhower warned publicly of the danger of communism in the region spreading by a **domino effect**; however, after much discussion within the administration and faced with substantial Congressional opposition led by Senator **Lyndon B. Johnson**, Eisenhower decided not to intervene militarily, and the French troops were forced to surrender. Attendees at a conference in Geneva in 1954 decided to free Laos and Cambodia immediately and to arrange a temporary division of Vietnam until free elections could be held to reunite the country. The United States, which was not a signatory to the agreement, then encouraged the leaders of the southern part of Vietnam not to agree to such elections, since it was clear that Ho Chi Minh would emerge victorious. Instead, the United States gave anticommunist **Ngo Dinh Diem** financial aid and promised more help in the future. In 1955, Diem won the presidency in elections in which he faced only limited opposition. Between 1954 and 1959, the United States sent over $2.3 billion to South Vietnam and also sent military advisers to help train **ARVN** (Army of the Republic of Viet Nam) troops. However, **Vietcong** guerilla forces, with aid from North Vietnam and China, steadily spread their control over most rural sections of the country, leaving the government influential only in urban areas. The government itself proved ineffective and failed to carry out promised reforms.

In 1954, the United States joined with Great Britain, France, Australia, New Zealand, Pakistan, Thailand, and the Philippines in establishing the **Southeast Asia Treaty Organization** (SEATO). Though modeled after NATO, this treaty did not require the signatories to regard an attack on one as an attack on all.

The following year, the United States was faced with a dilemma when the People's Republic of China ("Red China") began to shell two small offshore islands, **Quemoy** and **Matsu**, which were claimed by the nationalist Chinese on Taiwan. The question of whether this necessitated "massive retaliation" was avoided when the Chinese stopped shelling the islands.

The Middle East also presented the United States with a series of concerns. In 1948, Great Britain ended its mandate over Palestine, and, fulfilling a pledge made during World War I (the **Balfour Declaration**), provided land for a Jewish homeland. Jews in the area immediately declared the existence of **Israel** and were attacked by Arab forces. The United States recognized the new nation at once and provided it with material assistance. In 1949, the United Nations worked out an uneasy truce.

In 1955, the **Baghdad Pact** tied the United States together with Iraq, Iran, and Pakistan, in a mutual assistance agreement, and America also had an alliance with Saudi Arabia. However, the United States did not meet with the same success in Egypt. In 1954, Great Britain withdrew the troops that had been patrolling the **Suez Canal**. The United States had been attempting to win over Egyptian leader Col. **Gamal Abdel Nasser**, promising him, among other things, funds to build the enormous Aswan Dam across the Nile River. However, in September of 1955, Nasser entered into an agreement with the Soviet Union that called for the Soviet Union to supply large quantities of military equipment in return for Egyptian cotton. Secretary of State Dulles responded to this new threat to Israel by withdrawing the offer of American aid; in retaliation, Nasser "nationalized" the Suez Canal and announced that henceforth the tolls would be used to finance the dam. Western nations were alarmed, since much of their oil was shipped through the canal, though England and France favored a much more stern reply than the United States did.

In October of 1956, Israel, fearing the ever-increasing military capability of Egypt, launched a preemptive strike; the following day, Great Britain and France, fearing for the canal, invaded Egypt, but not before the canal was closed by sunken ships. The United States failed to support its two allies, joining instead with the Soviet Union in condemning this intervention in a United Nations debate. In November, a truce was worked out. Egypt remained in control of the canal, forbidding ships carrying goods to and from Israel from using it. In 1957, President Eisenhower announced the **Eisenhower Doctrine**. Expanding the scope of the Truman Doctrine, Eisenhower announced that the United States would use force if necessary to protect countries in the Middle East from communist aggression.

Preoccupied with Europe, Asia, and the Middle East, the United States paid little attention to Latin America. Resentment in the region surfaced when, in 1958, Vice President Nixon faced hostile crowds in a visit to Peru. In 1959, a Cuban revolutionary named **Fidel Castro** forced Cuban strongman Batista from power. At first, Americans viewed Castro as a patriot in the mold of George Washington and Simón Bolívar; he was hailed as a conquering hero during a visit to the United States shortly after his victory. However, by 1960, Castro had moved Cuba into the Soviet camp and had confiscated large quantities of American property. By January of 1962, the United States had severed diplomatic relations with Cuba, and a training area for anti-Castro forces had been established secretly in Guatemala.

In the **election of 1960**, Eisenhower's popularity gave considerable support to Richard Nixon, though Ike himself was only lukewarm toward his vice president. Nixon won the Republican nomination easily. The Democrats, on the other hand, had a large number of candidates. In a close race, Massachusetts Catholic **John F. Kennedy** barely won out over Texan **Lyndon B. Johnson**. To balance the ticket, Kennedy then offered Johnson the vice presidential spot. At first it seemed that Nixon, with the prestige and visibility of the vice presidency behind him, would be an easy victor; however, a series of televised debates permitted Kennedy to draw even. The result was a hairline victory for Kennedy (34,227,096 to 34,108,546).

In his "Farewell Address," President Eisenhower defended his administration's policies, but he warned the nation of the dangers of the growing **military-industrial complex**.

# "New Frontier," "Great Society," and Vietnam
# (1960–1968)

## The "New Frontier" of John F. Kennedy

In 1961, John F. Kennedy became the second-youngest president of the United States. In his inaugural address, he called upon the nation to make sacrifices for the good of the country and the world, challenging Americans to conquer "the New Frontier." His cabinet showed a balance among the various interest groups of the country, although the selection of his younger brother Robert as Attorney General was controversial. Both Houses of Congress had a majority of Democrats, but a coalition of Republicans and southern Democrats often blocked passage of administration bills.

Kennedy did achieve some legislative success. The **Housing Act of 1961** provided funds for increased federal housing and also for the development of mass-transit systems, and the **Peace Corps**, under the directorship of Kennedy in-law Sargent Shriver, proved remarkably successful in exporting American know-how to underdeveloped nations. But many proposals remained bottled up in Congress.

In 1961, the Soviet Union, ignoring suggestions that the superpowers cooperate in space exploration, put **Yuri Gagarin** into orbit as the first "cosmonaut." President Kennedy responded with the pledge to put a man on the moon before the end of the decade, and Congress made available necessary funding for **Project Apollo**. In February 1962, astronaut **John Glenn** made three orbits around the earth, and, in July of 1969, after nine more flights, *Apollo 11* successfully touched down on the moon and then returned to earth. The decade also saw the development of an entire series of telecommunications and spy satellites, raising questions as to the military potential of space.

In 1961, the **Twenty-Third Amendment** to the Constitution brought "home-rule" to the nation's capital, to the satisfaction of the overwhelmingly Black majority. Another constitutional development was the Supreme Court decision in *Baker v. Carr* in 1962, which declared that all state legislatures had to draw their voting districts so that each had approximately the same relative population ("one man, one vote"). In the 1964 decision of *Reynolds v. Sims*, the same requirement was applied to the federal House of Representatives.

The rights of minorities, a voting block that had played an important role in the 1960 election, received attention. Aided by provisions of the **Civil Rights Act of 1957**, a series of voting registration drives took place throughout the South; in addition, **sit-ins** at segregated eating and other commercial facilities focused the attention of the nation on racism. Many northerners rode **Freedom Buses** south to participate in demonstrations, often ignoring discrimination in their own backyards. A symbolic act took place when, with the help of federal troops, **James Meredith** was finally enrolled in the all-white University of Mississippi. In August of 1963, at a massive rally near the Lincoln Memorial in Washington, D.C., Dr. Martin Luther King spoke of his dreams for the American society.

In 1962, President Kennedy, in an effort to keep inflation to a minimum, persuaded steelworkers to accept a new contract with only a modest salary increase; soon thereafter, the major steel companies announced substantial increases in the prices of their products. Using all the leverage of the national government, Kennedy was able to compel the corporations to repeal their price increases; however, in so doing he lost considerable support in the business community.

Secretary of Defense **Robert McNamara** accepted the principle that the nuclear capabilities of the two superpowers provided a **mutual deterrent** to their use; however, he became convinced that the United States needed a "counterinsurgency force" to put out "brushfires" around the world. The United States also showed itself increasingly tolerant of nations wishing to remain neutral. Immediately upon taking office, Kennedy was faced with the decision of whether or not to permit a planned invasion of Cuba by anti-Castro forces. Convinced by American intelligence sources that the invasion would set off a popular uprising within Cuba, Kennedy gave his approval, but he refused to provide American air cover. The invasion of the **Bay of Pigs** was a disaster: there was no uprising, and Castro's surprisingly efficient army quickly overcame the invaders. The United States eventually ransomed those captured. In an attempt to counter Castro's influence in the rest of Latin America, Kennedy announced an **Alliance for Progress** for the region, similar to the Marshall Plan. However, the program received only minimal funding from Congress.

In June of 1961, Kennedy and Soviet Premier Khrushchev met in Vienna. The resolution of the Berlin issue was discussed; Khrushchev threatened to turn over control of the access roads to West Berlin to the East German authorities. In August of 1961, the communists suddenly began construction of the **Berlin Wall**, dividing the city in half.

Southeast Asia also remained in the news, as fighting between South Vietnam and the Vietcong continued. Kennedy increased American financial and material aid and also sent more military advisers to train the ARVN troops. There were approximately 15,000 U.S. advisers in Vietnam at the time of his death.

In the fall of 1961, alarmed about the success of the Soviet program, the United States resumed its underground testing of nuclear weapons.

In October of 1962, American spy planes provided indisputable photographic evidence that several missile installations were being constructed in Cuba. After weighing the options available, President Kennedy declared a quarantine zone around Cuba and announced that United States naval authorities would board and search all foreign ships bound for Cuba, turning back those with offensive weapons. The world stood on the brink of war in what was called the **Cuban Missile Crisis**. After a week, both sides drew back—the Soviet Union removed its missiles, and Kennedy pledged not to invade Cuba. Later, the United States also withdrew land-based missiles located in Turkey; these had become largely obsolete as a result of the increased deployment of nuclear submarines.

1963 saw some thawing of relations between the superpowers. The two nations signed an agreement prohibiting atomic testing in the atmosphere, and they also negotiated a substantial wheat sale.

In Europe, the strength of the NATO alliance was brought into question when French president **Charles de Gaulle** moved to create his own nuclear force and made it clear that he intended to pursue an independent foreign policy.

In November of 1963, John Kennedy was on a political trip through the South when he was assassinated in Dallas, Texas. Within two days, his alleged assassin, **Lee Harvey Oswald**, was in turn assassinated by **Jack Ruby** amidst growing questions of whether Oswald had actually operated alone. The **Warren Commission**, which investigated the assassination, reported that there was no conspiracy involved; however, doubts continued.

## Lyndon B. Johnson and the "Great Society"

In the public sympathy that followed Kennedy's death, President Johnson saw an opportunity to press forward to achieve a **Great Society**. In 1964, he declared **War on Poverty**, and Congress authorized the **Office of Economic Opportunity**, providing job retraining for those without work. Congress also enacted a Kennedy-sponsored tax cut that stimulated the economy, and established the **Volunteers in Service to America** program (VISTA), a domestic Peace Corps.

In the **election of 1964**, the nation was faced with a clear choice between moderate Johnson, with his liberal vice presidential candidate **Hubert Humphrey** of Minnesota, and conservative Senator **Barry Goldwater**, backed by a variety of right-wing groups, such as Robert Welch's **John Birch Society**. The result was a Johnson/Humphrey landslide, and Johnson felt, with justification, that he had a mandate to continue his legislative program.

In 1965, the United States adopted the long-debated **Medicare** program in the Medicare-Social Security Act; Congress also passed the **Elementary and Secondary Education Act**, which provided financial support for both public and private schools. The **Immigration Act of 1965**, did away with national quotas for immigrants that favored those from Northern European countries and instead placed the emphasis on the education and vocational skills of those seeking to come to the United States. The second in a series of **Clean Air Acts** was passed (the others being in 1963 and 1970). In 1966, in recognition of growing transit problems, the **Department of Transportation** was created and given cabinet status.

During these years, the country's population continued both to grow and to shift. In 1967, the Census Bureau announced that the country had reached the 200 million mark. It was also clear that the flight from farm to city and from Northeast to the South and especially the West was continuing.

Several interest groups made it clear that they did not feel they were sharing in the general prosperity of America's majority. In 1965, **Cesar Chavez** began an extended series of strikes aimed at organizing the migrant farm workers of the Southwest; much of his attention was focused on California's grape growers. America's Indians, or Native Americans, as some of them preferred to be called, sought increased **Red Power**; in 1969, an Indian group seized the abandoned prison on Alcatraz Island to publicize their goals. In 1966, women's rights activist **Betty Friedan** organized the **National Organization of Women** (NOW) to press her demands for greater equality and opportunity for women.

Black Americans continue to push for their rights. In a largely symbolic gesture, the **Twenty-Fourth Amendment** to the Constitution, ratified in 1964, prohibited the **poll tax**, which had been used in earlier times to discourage Black voting. Many civil rights groups, among them the **Congress for Racial Equality** (CORE) and the **Student Nonviolent Coordinating Committee** (SNCC), began to press for "Black Power," seeking immediate transfer of both political and economic power to Black Americans. The **Black Muslim** movement went so far as to call for the establishment of an independent Black American nation within the borders of the United States.

These groups began to put pressure on Dr. Martin Luther King's **Southern Christian Leadership Conference** (SCLC), which was making more moderate proposals for reform.

The **Civil Rights Act of 1964**, proclaimed a memorial to President Kennedy, added greater protection for minorities who wanted to vote and also prohibited discrimination in public accommodations and private employment. This act went beyond Constitutional prohibitions against discrimination, which apply only to the actions of governmental agencies, not to those of private individuals or institutions. The **Voting Rights Act of 1965** provided for federal inspection of any district in which literacy tests were still employed or where only a small number of the adult population actually took part in elections. Despite these measures, in 1965, racial violence erupted in **Selma, Alabama**, and elsewhere, and in August of the same year, a major riot broke out in the **Watts** section of Los Angeles.

Racially motivated riots continued to plague the nation for the following several years, most notably in Chicago and Cleveland in 1966 and Detroit in 1967. In 1968, the **Commission on Civil Disorders** acknowledged the problems faced by minorities within the nation and called for massive federal aid to overcome the problem. However, the exploding expense of the Vietnam War limited the funds available. In April 1968, the civil rights movement received a great shock when Dr. Martin Luther King was assassinated. Congress was quickly pressured into passing the **Civil Rights Act of 1968**, which forbade discrimination in the sale or rental of most housing.

## The Vietnam War

The civil strife in Vietnam entered a new phase in August of 1964 when it was announced to Congress that North Vietnamese warships had fired upon United States destroyers. The government later admitted that these destroyers had been electronically monitoring North Vietnam troop movement, and the entire legitimacy of the report to Congress on this incident has subsequently been called into question. Nevertheless, President Johnson ordered aerial retaliation, and Congress overwhelmingly passed the **Gulf of Tonkin Resolution**, which authorized the president to use whatever force necessary to "prevent further aggression" in the region. In 1965, President Diem was overthrown and killed by forces loyal to **General Nguyen Van Thieu**, with at least tacit American approval. American troops began to flood into South Vietnam: in 1965, the number rose from 23,000 to more than 180,000; in 1966, the number rose to 360,000; and by 1967, more than a half million U.S. troops were involved in the conflict.

The war had an immediate impact at home. Not only did millions of American males have to search their consciences when it came time to register for the draft, with many fleeing to Canada rather than serving in what they considered to be an immoral war, but television brought the horrors of the war into every home daily on the evening news. Throughout the United States, an increasing number of demonstrations were held protesting American involvement in the fighting. A series of optimistic bulletins from official sources encouraged Americans to believe that success was just around the corner. However, a massive **Tet Offensive** against South Vietnamese urban centers early in 1968 undermined many Americans' confidence in what their government was saying. On March 31, 1968, in a televised address, President Johnson ordered a halt to the extensive American bombing of North Vietnam and asked the North Vietnamese government to participate in negotiations to end the hostilities. He also announced that he would not run for reelection in the fall. By May, negotiations had begun in Paris; however, the fighting continued.

# The Nixon Presidency and its Aftermath (1968–1976)

As early as 1967, Senator **Eugene McCarthy** had begun to campaign for president, taking as his major issue his opposition to the Vietnamese war. With support from many younger Americans, he made a surprisingly strong showing, with 42 percent of the vote against the incumbent president of his own party in the New Hampshire primary and comparable strength in other informal polls. Early in 1968, **Robert Kennedy** also declared his candidacy; however, Kennedy was assassinated in June just after winning the important California primary.

Vice President Hubert Humphrey had not entered the race until learning that President Johnson did not intend to run for reelection. However, he then campaigned strenuously. The **Democratic Convention in Chicago** was marked by dissension within the hall and rioting outside in the streets as Chicago police battled crowds of picketers before national television cameras. Humphrey was nominated on the first ballot, but the party was badly split, especially by Governor **George Wallace** of Alabama. Wallace had gained attention in 1964 for his efforts to block racial integration in his home state. Now his message was aimed at northern working class voters, who felt anger and distrust at social radicalism and liberal reform alike. Leaving the Democratic Party to run on his own American Independent ticket, he received just under 10 million votes in the general election. Thus, Wallace cost Humphrey some support from the right wing of his party, while many supporters of McCarthy or Robert Kennedy to the left also refused to support Humphrey.

In contrast, Richard Nixon, who had been quietly campaigning for several years, was the overwhelming choice of the Republicans; he selected as his running mate Governor **Spiro Agnew** of Maryland. Appealing for support from the **Silent Majority**, Nixon promised to "bring the American people together." Nixon refused to participate in any televised debates. Although he was far behind initially, Humphrey closed the gap toward the end. Even so, Nixon and Agnew emerged victorious.

### Nixon's Domestic Policies

Nixon assumed the presidency of a troubled nation. Early promise of the Civil Rights movement had soured as frustrated Blacks looked more to the militance of **Malcolm X** or the **Black Panthers** than the peaceful moderation advocated by Martin Luther King. King's assassination in April 1968 had sent a storm of urban riots across the country. King's killing along with the assassination of Robert Kennedy in June of that same year caused many Americans to feel the society itself was coming unhinged. For increasing numbers of people, the violence at home seemed a direct echo of the unwarranted violence the nation was causing in Vietnam. Some of the sharpest criticism of American society came from young middle-class students, often organized on college campuses by the **Students for a Democratic Society** (SDS). The SDS had been formed in 1962 with the issuing of the **Port Huron Statement**, which condemned what it saw as the development of the United States into a vast bureaucratic establishment insensitive to the needs of individual citizens. While the Port Huron Statement itself drew only limited public attention, it quickly expanded into the **Free Speech Movement** at the University of California at Berkeley in 1964 and became a focus for national concern. This was the first time that America encountered its own youth as an organized voice for social dissent, and the impact shook the country's self-confidence, especially as student protest began to focus on the Vietnam War.

Although he could not ease the profound national distress, Nixon proved able to harness it politically. Sensing that the liberal consensus formed around the New Frontier and the Great Society had begun to unravel, he emphasized "law and order" over governmental efforts at social reform, tapping into a considerable amount of support in the population. While he did not dismantle the Great Society's large governmental agencies, he used them with restraint and less enthusiasm than his predecessor. Influenced by a controversial 1965 report by **Daniel Patrick Moynihan** arguing that problems among poor blacks stemmed more from the break-up of families than poverty itself, Nixon took the position that the nation would benefit from a period of "benign neglect" on the subject of race; and he moved to end forced busing of students to achieve racial balance in urban public schools. Nixon also made an effort to reshape the Supreme Court through the appointment of conservative justices.

Southern Democrats were often conservative in outlook and particularly distressed by the recent Civil Rights initiatives of Kennedy and Johnson. Nixon and his Republican advisors sensed that "the solid South" could be broken up and lured in significant numbers from the Democratic to the Republican Party, which the South had shunned since the days of Reconstruction. This **Southern Strategy** proved successful and brought about a historic realignment of the two political parties.

### Nixon and Vietnam

Nixon's interest as a president lay less in domestic affairs than foreign policy, where he wrestled above all with the problem of how to extricate the nation from Vietnam. He saw United States involvement there as fruitless and was well aware of the rising public objection to the war. On the other hand, he had had the reputation throughout his career as a tough anticommunist and was unwilling to be the first American president to preside over a losing war. He and his National Security Advisor (later Secretary of State), **Henry Kissinger**, formulated the policy of **Vietnamization**. This policy stated that United States ground troops would leave Vietnam, reducing American casualties and, they hoped, reducing domestic criticism of the war effort. At the same time, American air power would use bombing to force North Vietnam to negotiate on terms that would bring "peace with honor" for the United States.

Despite this policy, events in the war continued to demoralize the nation. In October of 1969, while peace talks bogged down in Paris, war protestors organized **Vietnam Moratorium Day**. Two hundred fifty thousand demonstrators marched past the White House, while Nixon resolutely watched a football game on television. Early in the following year, the American people were appalled to read of the 1968 massacre of the entire Vietnamese village of **My Lai** by United States Army troops. In the spring of 1970, Nixon ordered troops to cross the border from Vietnam into neutral Cambodia to pursue North Vietnamese guerrillas who were using that country as a safe haven. There was public outcry at this expansion of the war. On May 4, National Guardsmen sent to control a student protest at **Kent State University** in Ohio fired on the crowd, killing four students.

Nonetheless, Nixon stuck to his policies. In an October speech shortly before the 1972 elections, Henry Kissinger stated, "Peace is at hand." However, by late December, Nixon was sending heavy bombing missions over North Vietnam and, in 1972, ordered the mining of Haiphong Harbor. At the same time, in a bold stroke of foreign policy, he began negotiations for better relations with both the Soviet Union and Communist China. His historic visit to China was particularly remarkable, for he was the first president to open communications with that nation since its communist government took power in 1949. These overtures threatened to undercut North Vietnam's base of support and led to more serious negotiations in Paris.

In January of 1973, it was agreed that United States troops would pull out of Vietnam altogether when American prisoners of war had been returned. This agreement seemed to preserve some measure of American dignity. However, on the day in 1975 when the last United States helicopter carried personnel off the roof of the U.S. Embassy in Saigon, leaving thousands of South Vietnamese allies behind as North Vietnamese troops streamed into the capital, it was difficult to avoid the awareness of an American defeat.

## Watergate

In the fall of 1972, with the Vietnam debacle still in the future, the China maneuver fresh in mind, and progress beginning in the Paris talks, there was some easement to the war protest, and Nixon's domestic policies were finding a solid base of support. In an election landslide that year, he defeated **George McGovern**, a candidate from the most liberal wing of the Democratic Party, winning every state except Massachusetts. Despite the strength of Nixon's campaign, members of his reelection team engaged in a series of dirty tricks, often illegal, to undermine and spy on the Democrats. Such activities had begun during Nixon's first term. Suspicious and hostile to any form of criticism, he had formed a group called **the plumbers**, who used techniques of espionage to infiltrate and disrupt any group seen as opposition to the president. These matters reached public attention in June of 1972, when five men were caught at night going through files and installing bugging devices at the Democratic National Committee Headquarters in the **Watergate**, a hotel and office complex in Washington, DC. At first, it appeared that the break-in would pass as an isolated incident, but investigative work by **Washington Post** reporters **Bob Woodward** and **Carl Bernstein** began to reveal a web of involvement that spiraled higher and higher into Nixon's administration until it reached the president himself. Though no one suspected that he had personally devised the Watergate break-in, the possibility grew that he had directed a cover-up of the incident while assuring the public that he had no knowledge of the affair at all. The situation became focused, as one prominent Republican senator put it, on the question, "What did the president know, and when did he know it?"

Pressure on Nixon intensified when it was learned that he had personal tape recordings of his White House meetings throughout the period. When demands were made for the tapes to be produced, Nixon refused. Hoping to defuse the criticism rising about him, he allowed the appointment of **Archibald Cox** as an independent prosecutor for the Watergate break-in case. However, when Cox also demanded the tapes, Nixon fired him, bringing on a storm of public protest. Cox's successor, **Leon Jawarski**, repeated the demand, as did the Judiciary Committee of the House of Representatives, which began inquiries into whether there were grounds to impeach the president. The issue of the tapes went before the Supreme Court, which ruled unanimously that Nixon must relinquish them. In August of 1974, the tapes revealed that Nixon had taken a direct role in hindering the Watergate investigation. Facing the certainty of impeachment, Nixon resigned the presidency on August 8, 1974.

Late in the previous year, Vice President **Spiro Agnew** had resigned in the face of his own scandal involving tax fraud and the acceptance of bribes while governor of Maryland. Nixon had appointed **Gerald Ford**, the minority leader of the House of Representatives, to be vice-president in his place. Thus, after Nixon's own resignation, Gerald Ford became the first person to serve as both vice-president and president without having been elected to either post.

In the midst of the Watergate tension in 1973, the Supreme Court took on an equally difficult issue. In the case of ***Roe v. Wade***, a 7–2 majority followed the position of Justice **Harry Blackmun**, striking down a Texas antiabortion law on the grounds that abortion was a woman's federally protected right under the Constitution. Greeted with jubilation by some and horror by others, that decision polarized an issue that remains unsettled.

# From Carter to Reagan
# (1976–1980)

The presidential election of 1976 was a close race in which Gerald Ford was defeated by **Jimmy Carter**, a political newcomer only part of the way through his first term as governor of Georgia, and the first Southern Democrat to be elected president since before the Civil War. To a public demoralized by the Watergate revelations, Carter's status as an outsider seemed refreshing, particularly as he began with hopes of making government more efficient and honest. Once in office, however, he found that his inexperience and lack of political connections within the Washington system left him unable to carry his policies forward.

Carter's troubles worsened when **OPEC** (Organization of Petroleum Exporting Countries) began collectively to hike up the price of oil on which the United States was heavily dependent. Businesses and organizations throughout the country felt the strain as costs for basic heating and transportation skyrocketed. The prices for standard goods rose along with those costs, and the rate of inflation grew from 6 percent to 14 percent between 1977 and 1979. Carter could do little but object to the OPEC rates and urge Americans to lower their thermostats to 65 degrees. Though he saw the need to revise the nation's energy policies and reduce dependence on imported oil, Carter could make little headway with these issues in Congress.

In 1978, the Supreme Court addressed a case that signaled a shift from the mid-1960s in the federal government's approach to racial inequality. **Allan Bakke**, a white applicant who had been denied admission to the University of California at Davis medical school, sued the Regents of the University of California on the grounds that lesser qualified minority candidates had been admitted under **affirmative action** to meet the university's racial quotas. In an ambiguously worded 5–4 decision, the Court ruled that quotas were illegal and that Bakke should be admitted. However, the decision went on to say that race could continue to be a factor in admissions, without specific quotas, for an organization wishing to attain racial diversity in its make-up.

Foreign affairs brought Carter his greatest success and also some intense frustrations. He brought **Anwar el-Sadat** of Egypt and **Menachem Begin** of Israel together for 13 days at **Camp David**, the presidential retreat in Maryland, and helped them reach an agreement ending a long-standing state of war between those two nations. However, his efforts to achieve **Salt II**, an arms control treaty with the Soviet Union, were thwarted by cold war supporters among Senate Republicans. In 1979, the Shah of Iran, long supported by the United States, was over-thrown by Islamic fundamentalists under the **Ayatollah Ruholla Khomeini**. In retaliation for the American role in the Shah's regime, Khomeini seized the U.S. Embassy in Teheran and took 53 Americans hostage, holding them until the final day of Carter's presidency. As the hostage situation dragged on through 1980, it seemed to typify Carter's inability to assert effective leadership at home or abroad.

In the **election of 1980**, Republican **Ronald Reagan** defeated Jimmy Carter by a significant margin. The issues between the two were clearly drawn, for Reagan ran with the intention of reversing patterns of government that had become traditional since Franklin Roosevelt's defeat of Herbert Hoover in 1932. His goals were to loosen restrictions on capitalist growth, to reduce the size and scope of the federal government, and to cut back on federal taxation. There was more support for these domestic policies than at any time since the New Deal. As a result, the Reagan election marks a significant turning point in American political history. In foreign affairs, Reagan advocated increased spending for military defense, with a vigorous cold war posture toward the Soviet Union and communism anywhere else in the world. Aside from his specific policies, Reagan represented the return to an attitude of confidence and pride in America as the world's preeminent nation. There were some who questioned the wisdom of that attitude. But as a veteran actor with a jaunty, candid manner, Reagan projected his message with great appeal, and a country worn down by 15 years of strife, failure, and disillusionment was eager to receive it.

# Reagan and Bush
# (1980-1992)

### Reagan's "New Federalism"

Speaking confidently of "a new morning in America," Reagan set out energetically with a domestic agenda to reduce the role of the federal government in favor of state and local control. Central to his strategy was "**supply-side economics**" (or "Reaganomics" as some skeptically put it). Lower taxes put more money into the control of wealthy individuals and corporations, which were then expected to expand and produce more, thus revitalizing the economy. A welcome corollary to lowered taxes was the reduction of federal expenses. Environmental protections were rolled back under the enthusiastic leadership of Secretary of the Interior **James Watts**. Federal social programs were cut back and the responsibility for them was shifted to the state and local levels. Unlike the federal government, however, most state and local governments were constitutionally required to operate within an annually balanced budget, so they were not in a good position to take up these social burdens. Many of the poorer members of the population faced circumstances more painful during the 1980s than at any time since the Great Depression.

Reagan's supply-side economic philosophy went hand in hand with the desire to give a freer rein to business management. In 1981 he engaged in a highly publicized showdown with the **Air Traffic Controllers Union**, firing hundreds of them on the grounds that it was illegal for them to strike and forcing them to back down on their contract demands. Labor union membership throughout the nation declined dramatically in the 1980s. At the same time there was a movement to ease federal regulations controlling business practices. In the **savings and loans** banking industry, officials responded to deregulation with reckless expansion and speculative investment. The extent of their irresponsibility was a public scandal, and the government had to intervene to prevent an entire collapse of the industry at a cost of $500 billion by 1990.

While his domestic policies aimed at shrinking the size of federal government, Reagan also called for a dramatic **increase in military spending**. The cost of these programs coupled with the reduced tax revenues of his supply-side economics created the largest national debt in U.S. history. In 1980 the debt was averaged at $4000 per capita of taxpayers. By 1989 it had more than tripled to $12,500.

The impact of Regan's economic policies varied greatly from one segment of the society to another. After a severe recession in 1981 and 1982, the mid-1980s were boom times for the wealthy, particularly those working directly in the financial markets, and some of them showed their new prosperity ostentatiously. In 1976 the richest 1% of the population had owned 18% of the nation's wealth. By 1989 that figure had become 36% and was still rising into the 1990s. At the same time the urban poor were strapped by the shrinkage of federal support programs. In rural areas there were numerous foreclosures on smaller farmers who could not meet their debts. Despite the social tensions inherent in the situation, the majority of Americans felt the country was on an upswing from the despondency of the 1970s. Whatever complaints were leveled at his policies, none of them seemed to touch Reagan's enormous personal popularity. He came to be referred to as "the teflon president," since all criticism seemed to slide away from him effortlessly.

The assertion of a conservative philosophy in government and economics was matched in the area of social values. In the area of civil rights, Reagan's Justice Dept. actively sought to undo affirmative action decisions designed to improve minority representation in education and employment opportunities. Television evangelists such as **Rev. Jerry Falwell** and **Rev. Pat Robertson** spoke for what they termed "**the Moral Majority**" and called for a return to their vision of "family values." They brought political pressure to bear particularly on an effort to reverse the Supreme Court's 1973 *Roe v. Wade* decision defending the right to abortion and its stance against prayer in public schools.

The concept of "family values," however, proved elusive to apply in a society whose practices of family life had changed a great deal since the post-World War II years. The composition of the population as a whole was shifting, in part under the influence of the Immigration Act of 1965, which removed quotas that had favored western European nations. Blacks, Hispanics, Asians and Native Americans comprised 25% of the population by the end of the 1980s. During that decade, 37% of U.S. immigration came from Asia; 47% came from Mexico, the Caribbean and Latin America. Within the family itself, single parent households had risen from 11% in 1960 to 25% by 1990. Even in two-parent households, both husband and wife were far likelier to have jobs, relying on day-care services for their children. Heterosexual couples living together unmarried had become a commonplace, and the society was moving toward an easier acceptance of homosexual relationships as well. For some, these developments were precisely the reason traditional family values needed forceful reassertion. Others thought it more reasonable that "family values" should reflect the values of those actually living in the families.

**Foreign policy under Reagan**

Reagan adopted a vigorous anticommunism in his foreign policy, seeking to move away from the mood of defeatism in the country following the Vietnam War. He publicly referred to the Soviet Union as an "evil empire" and put enormous pressure on them by escalating military expenditures. The Soviets were especially alarmed in 1984 by his pursuit of the **Strategic Defense Initiative (SDI)**, a controversial plan to use satellites as a defensive screen against incoming missiles, labeled "Star Wars" by skeptics.

Meanwhile American forces suffered a painful loss in Lebanon. Israel had invaded this country on its northern border in 1982, trying to dislodge Palestinian opposition fighters harbored there. The U.S. sent a detachment of marines to act as peacekeepers, but they became targets themselves. A suicide bomber drove a truck full of explosives into the gate of the U.S. barracks, killing 241 marines. After a short time, Reagan withdrew the American troops.

The administration's direct action against communism focused mainly on Latin America. In 1983 troops were sent to oust a new Marxist leader from the tiny island of Grenada in the Caribbean, and the U.S. gave support to the government of El Salvador as it waged an ongoing civil war against leftist forces. However, the most heated area for Reagan in Central America was **Nicaragua**. In 1979 a regime corrupt but friendly to the U.S. was overthrown by a group calling themselves the **Sandinistas**, in memory of a resistance leader of the 1930s. President Carter had originally offered friendly relations to the Sandinistas, but as their communist leanings became more evident, the Reagan administration viewed them as enemies. The CIA supported a force called the **Contras**, which undertook an ongoing but unsuccessful effort to depose the Sandinistas.

Public opinion in the U.S. began to grow alarmed at this development, fearing that the country could become enmeshed in another Vietnam experience. Criticism became acute when it was revealed in 1984 that the CIA had planted mines in Managua, Nicaragua's principal harbor. Soon afterward Congress voted to cut off funding for the Contras and proscribed any further support for them by law.

## Second term problems

As the **election of 1984** approached, it was clear that the Republicans would nominate the Ronald Reagan / George Bush ticket for a second term. Among the Democrats the front runner, former Vice President **Walter Mondale**, had stiff competition from **Gary Hart**, a young senator from Colorado. The charismatic black leader **Rev. Jesse Jackson** was also a powerful factor in the primaries. However, Mondale secured the nomination and made the striking move of selecting as his running mate New York congresswoman **Geraldine Ferraro**, the first woman to run on a national ticket in a presidential election. Mondale campaigned in the hope that inconsistencies and tensions in the Reagan policies would come to the fore. However, the appeal of Reagan's reassertion of national pride and his own great popularity proved unshakable. Although Democrats showed well in the congressional elections, Reagan himself swept back into office in a landslide, winning every state except Mondale's own Minnesota and the District of Columbia.

Despite his convincing re-election, Reagan encountered serious difficulties in his second term. Several members of his administration were forced to resign because of questionable financial dealings, most prominently his outspoken Attorney General **Edwin Meese**. In his first term Reagan had made the well regarded appointment of **Sandra Day O'Connor** as the first woman to serve as a Justice on the Supreme Court. Now, however, dissension between conservatives and liberals flared up as he nominated **Robert J. Bork** to fill another vacancy on the bench. Bork's legal credentials were impressive, but his firmly conservative stand on judicial issues and his extensive writings made him an alarming prospect to many. After several weeks of acrimonious debate carried on in the public spotlight, the Senate refused to confirm Bork. Reagan reluctantly withdrew his name and replaced him with **Anthony Kennedy**, a judge of conservative leanings but a less contentious manner. This episode highlighted an increasing trend toward politicizing the judicial confirmation process.

Reagan's gravest problem came from his dealings in foreign affairs. When several Americans were kidnapped by radical Islamic groups in the Middle East, he declared firmly that he "would never negotiate with terrorists." However, in 1986 it was revealed that the administration had in fact been negotiating with Iran to intercede in return for the sale of arms. This embarrassing revelation then moved into an area of serious constitutional illegality, the **Iran-Contra Scandal**. It emerged that in an operation under the guidance of **Lt. Col. Oliver North**, a member of the National Security Council staff, proceeds from the Iranian arms sales were being funneled secretly to the Contras in Nicaragua, going behind the back of Congress's ban on continued support for those forces. Oliver North and National Security Advisor John Poindexter were found guilty of falsifying documents and lying to congress, though North in particular had become a hero to many conservatives. (Both men were subsequently pardoned by George Bush as president.) A disturbing question for the general public was Reagan's own degree of involvement in the scandal. He claimed that he had paid little attention to details of the operation at the time, and both he and Vice President Bush avoided direct censure. However, people found themselves with the unpleasant choice of a president who had willfully subverted the constitution or one who, as the oldest man ever to occupy the presidency, had lost his grip on the reins of his administration. (De-classified documents have subsequently indicated that Reagan was clearly engaged in the Iran-Contra operation.)

The luster of Reagan's presidency suffered another blow toward the end of his second term when in October, 1987 the stock market, which had been booming through the 1980s, experienced the sharpest one day drop in its history. This was not a crash but a readjustment of stock prices which had grown inflated during the exuberant, often speculative trading of the 80s. The market soon stabilized. Nonetheless, this financial shock added that much more force to public opinion polls expressing an increasing disenchantment with Reagan's brand of conservatism.

### The presidency of George Bush

Democrats approached **the election of 1988** with understandable optimism, though such leaders of the party as New York governor Mario Cuomo, New Jersey senator Bill Bradley and Massachusetts senator Edward Kennedy declined to run. The nomination fell to the relatively unknown Massachusetts governor **Michael Dukakis**. After some uncertainty in the early primaries, Vice President **George Bush** secured the Republican nomination. Public dissatisfaction with the end of Reagan's second term gave Dukakis a lead in opinion polls throughout the summer of the campaign. However, he proved a lackluster candidate, and his lead gradually dissipated. Meanwhile, under the guidance of his campaign manager **Lee Atwater**, Bush relentlessly pursued negative advertising and with considerable distortion attacked Dukakis as a liberal "soft on crime." Bush's campaign was widely regarded as one of the most discreditable of the century, but in the absence of effective countermeasures from his opponent, he won the election by a comfortable margin.

Bush undertook his presidency seriously hampered by the huge national debt he had inherited from Reagan. Despite the firm campaign promise, "Read my lips: no new taxes," he quickly found himself compelled to raise tax revenues. This move undermined his creditability with conservatives without making any noticeable improvement in the recession gripping the country. If there were obstacles in Bush's path toward active domestic legislation, he showed little interest in overcoming them. He spoke more about issues such as education or environmental protection than his predecessor had, but seemed content to settle for an unproductive stalemate or "gridlock" with the Democrats controlling Congress. There was less national legislation generated in the years of the Bush administration than in any other since Calvin Coolidge's.

In 1991, **Thurgood Marshall** retired from the bench of the Supreme Court. Marshall, the only black jurist appointed to the high court, had been the NAACP's key civil rights litigator and had argued the landmark *Brown v. the Board of Education of Topeka* case before the Supreme Court in 1954. In his place Bush nominated U.S. Appeals Court Judge **Clarence Thomas**, also a black, but a firm conservative whose legal credentials were not as distinguished as Marshall's. Thomas was in the midst of a bitterly contested confirmation struggle when a law professor named **Anita Hill** came forward with the charge that Thomas had sexually harassed her when she was working on his staff at the EEOC. Thomas was eventually confirmed, but the acrimony of the proceedings and the sordid detail of the testimony left him tarnished as well as the president and the members of the Senate Judiciary Committee.

Meanwhile in Los Angeles a black man named **Rodney King** sued members of the Los Angeles police department for their brutal beating of him during an arrest. The beating had been filmed on an amateur videotape which was aired across the nation to public disgust; yet in Los Angeles in April of 1992, an all-white jury acquitted the policemen. The city exploded in one of the worst race riots in the nation's history, but the Bush administration maintained a detached posture through the event.

If the Bush presidency was characterized by inertia at home, it was a time of stirring events abroad. In July of 1989 a movement of Chinese dissidents was violently crushed at **Tiananmen Square** in Beijing, but elsewhere in the world dramatic events had more positive outcomes. The anticommunist party **Solidarity** under the leadership of **Lek Walesa** succeeded after years of struggle in overcoming the pro-Soviet regime in Poland. Soviet control of East Germany cracked shortly after. The hated **Berlin Wall** was dismantled in November of 1989, and the Soviet Union itself came apart in the weeks following. In South Africa the white government renounced the long-standing policy of apartheid and freed black leader **Nelson Mandala**, whom they had held in prison for 27 years. Mandela became president of South Africa under a reformed constitution. In Latin America, the Sandinistas were voted out of power in Nicaragua, and civil strife eased in El Salvador. President Bush spoke with understandable optimism about the birth of "a new world order," though it was clear that this complex array of developments would bring its own new problems.

The Bush administration itself had declared a "war on drugs." This effort focused attention at one point on **Panama**, where **General Manuel Noriega** had been running an illicit drug traffic for years. This situation had been tolerated in the past, and indeed Noriega had at times worked closely with U.S. intelligence agencies. However, in December of 1989 U.S. forces entered Panama, captured Noriega and brought him back to Florida for trial, conviction and imprisonment.

In August of the following year, President **Saddam Hussein** of Iraq invaded the small neighboring country of Kuwait. As with Noriega, Hussein had had dealings with the U.S. in the recent past. His armed forces, the most formidable in the region, had been built up with American aid to provide opposition to Iran in a war that had gone on through most of the 1980s. With this move, however, he threatened to destabilize the region and gain leverage over a significant portion of the world's oil supply. Moving with speed and skill, Bush formed a coalition of Middle Eastern and European states as well as the United Nations against Saddam Hussein. Within a few days he launched operation "Desert Shield" to protect the border of Saudi Arabia. A month later, having secured congressional approval by a thin 5-vote margin, Bush began air attacks on Iraq, followed by operation "Desert Storm," which swiftly defeated Saddam's forces on the ground. Though some criticized Bush for stopping short of deposing Saddam Hussein altogether, the **Gulf War** on the whole had reached a resoundingly successful conclusion in a short time with remarkably few casualties. In the immediate aftermath of the war, Bush's approval rating in polls soared to above 90%. In the following weeks, however, the gridlock patterns of his administration returned, and his popularity had dwindled as the 1992 election drew near.

The **election of 1992** reflected an unusual level of ideological division and uncertainty among the American people. Some felt that Reagan's 1980 election had marked a turn away from fifty years of misguided public policy. In their view, the movement toward valid conservative principles was still in its formative stage and had to be pushed further. Within the Republican party, however, George Bush had failed to win the confidence of the far right. He faced stiff primary competition from **Pat Buchanan** and Rev. Pat Robertson. While his renomination was never really in doubt, he entered the campaign itself with a weakened base of support.

Many people on the other side were concerned by the social impact of the Reagan/Bush policies and wished to reverse, or at least to moderate, the conservative trend of the last twelve years. Governor **Bill Clinton** of Arkansas emerged as the leader of a new group called the **Democratic Leadership Council** who felt that their party, while retaining its liberal social outlook, had to move closer to the center in its economic policies if it was to challenge the Republicans successfully for the White House. Clinton's message proved politically persuasive, though he himself was a flawed messenger. He had used connections to avoid service in the Vietnam War. When accused of smoking marijuana while a Rhodes Scholar, he defended himself unconvincingly, saying he had tried it but "had not inhaled." He also had a string of extra-marital sexual affairs in his background. These issues of character plagued Clinton through a bitter primary struggle, but in the end he gained the nomination. The prestige of the Democratic ticket was significantly enhanced by the addition of Tennessee senator **Al Gore** for vice president.

While the ideological split between conservatives and liberals was more sharply etched than usual in American politics, paradoxically the level of public indifference or disaffection toward the political process was also high. Billionaire **Ross Perot**, spending $60 million of his own money, led a powerful third party campaign. His projected policies were not clearly stated, but many Americans shared his disgust for "politics as usual" and gravitated toward him as a protest against the gridlock and in-fighting of the two main parties.

Once nominated, Clinton was an effective campaigner, quick on his feet and often eloquent as a speaker, impressive in his ability to grasp the complex details of an array of issues, and a master at the informal setting of a series of televised "town meetings." **Hilary Clinton** proved an able partner to her husband, and it was clear that if he were elected, she would take on a more dynamic role in the government than was traditionally the case for First Ladies. Starting from behind in the polls, Clinton used his skills in debate and his relentless pounding on economic issues in the midst of a recession to win a close election. With 43% of the total, he failed to win a majority of the popular vote but finished comfortably ahead of Bush's 38%. Ross Perot gained 19% of the vote, the strongest third party showing in a presidential election since Theodore Roosevelt's Bull Moose Party in 1912.

Liberals greeted Clinton's defeat of Reagan/Bush Republicanism as the dawn of a new day. Conservatives saw it as a catastrophe. As events developed, it would prove to be neither. The character issues that had played such a role in the primary race would resurface as an increasingly dominant factor in Clinton's presidency itself, dulling the impact of his political leadership. The ambivalence between conservative and liberal values that had been stirred up by Ronald Reagan would continue to mark the nation's temperament for years to come.

# Index